Practically Vegan

Nisha Melvani

Practically Vegan

More Than 100 Easy, Delicious Vegan Dinners on a Budget

Foreword by
Jonathan Safran Foer

Photographs by
Dana Gallagher

Library of Congress
Cataloging-in-Publication Data
Names: Melvani, Nisha, author.
Title: Practically vegan : more than 100 easy,
    delicious vegan dinners on a budget / Nisha
    Melvani ; foreword by Jonathan Safran Foer.
Description: New York : Rodale, 2022. | Includes
    index.
Identifiers: LCCN 2021017743 (print) | LCCN
    2021017744 (ebook) | ISBN 9780593233405 |
    ISBN 9780593233412 (ebook)
Subjects: LCSH: Vegetarian cooking. | Vegan
    cooking. | Quick and easy cooking. | LCGFT:
    Cookbooks.
Classification: LCC TX837 .M523 2022 (print) |
    LCC TX837 (ebook) | DDC 641.5/636—dc23
LC record available at lccn.loc.gov/2021017743
LC ebook record available at lccn.loc.
    gov/2021017744

ISBN 978-0-593-23340-5
Ebook ISBN 978-0-593-23341-2

Printed in China

Book and cover design by Ian Dingman
Cover photographs by Dana Gallagher

10 9 8 7 6 5 4 3 2 1

First Edition

Anand, my caring partner, thank you for your unwavering support in life and throughout this process. You took on the lion's share of looking after our three daughters without hesitation. I'm so grateful for all you did—except for maybe the laundry. I didn't realize quite how color-blind you really are!

My SPAM-loving mom, thank you for encouraging me to pursue my love for vegetables even though you hate them! You bought me my first camera and sent me to culinary school, which is how all of this came to be.

Contents

HELP IS ON THE WAY

Jonathan
Safran Foer

It is fairly simple to *want* change in one's life, altogether possible to *make* change, and extremely difficult to *sustain* change.

It's embarrassing, maybe even shaming, to think of the promises we've made to ourselves: less screen time, more exercise, less one-click shopping, more reading. I've made all of those vows and enacted those changes, and then, fairly quickly, reverted to my old ways. Mark Twain supposedly said, "Giving up smoking is the easiest thing in the world. I know because I've done it thousands of times." It's not enough to have good intentions or even to act on those intentions. What matters is our ability to shape habits over time. Our lives are processes, not events.

I have wrestled with my eating habits since I was a child. Even as a nine-year-old I had strong instincts about what was "right" and "wrong" to eat. Over the years, those instincts have been shaped by information. I no longer think about eating in terms of moral binaries, but the implications of our eating choices couldn't be more profound, especially when it comes to eating animal products. It is not an exaggeration to say that the future of our planet depends on what we do and don't eat.

Relatively few people want to become vegetarians or vegans, but everyone wants to reduce the amount of destruction and suffering in the world. It is no one's opinion but scientific fact that reducing the amount of animal products we consume is one of the most powerful ways, as individuals, to reduce destruction and suffering. That doesn't mean that we have to change our identities. And it doesn't mean that our choice is between "going all the way" (as if anyone on earth were even capable of such perfection) and doing nothing at all. Our eating choices are essential parts of vast and vastly important cause-and-effect chains; making sensitive choices as often as possible will reduce the amount of destruction and suffering in the world.

That probably sounds obvious and easy, yet most people—myself very much included—find it difficult to sustain change. We need help. I was lucky enough to meet Nisha Melvani a couple of years ago. A friend turned me on to her Instagram feed, Cooking for Peanuts (@cookingforpeanuts), and in a great coincidence, our children go to the same school in Brooklyn. Nisha is passionate but never moralizing. She is creative, but in a way that is contagious rather than just impressive. She cooks as a nutritionist, chef, and advocate, but primarily as a mother. With an accessible, conversational approach, she shows how easy and pleasurable it can be to learn new ways of preparing food for ourselves and our loved ones. Her recipes are inexpensive, straightforward, and delicious. They have helped me change my life. And they will help you change yours.

The Cook Behind the Book

I tried to get out of writing this chapter. I told my editor, "They're here for the food. They don't want to know about me!" It turns out this chapter was non-negotiable. So, if you are here for just the food, that's totally cool. Skip ahead to Pantry Staples on page 15. That one you must read.

I'm trying to resist using the cliché "I always loved to cook." But the thing is, I really did always love to cook, just like I loved to sew and play the piano—I sound like one of those eighteenth-century girls being primed for marriage. My story, however, is anything but romantic.

I was born and raised on the island of Jamaica by two full-time working parents. So, in reality, they didn't really do much of the raising. It was Paulette, my awesome nanny, with whom I spent most of my time. She and I were very close, but she took no prisoners. If I was out of line, I was in big trouble. And I rarely toed the line.

It was a challenge for her to manage me. I was a capricious kid, very naughty, always wanting to try something new. Which explains why piano and sewing were eventually replaced by new ventures deemed far more interesting at the time. But cooking, that I never really did quit. Some part of me couldn't relinquish the challenge of transforming something as mundane as white flour into a delicious, crispy pizza.

My parents didn't cook. My mom ate because she had to. Her default foods were SPAM and "bun and cheese," a Jamaican specialty where the bun is a dried-fruit-spiced loaf, and the cheese is packaged as Tastee Cheese. I never saw my mom eat a fruit or vegetable, besides the occasional banana and the many sides of french fries. She recently had one foot of her colon removed because it was so damaged. I'm 100 percent sure it was 100 percent caused by her no-fiber diet, though she will never admit it.

My grandma was the best cook I've ever known. She was constantly humming Bob Marley tunes while cooking. Her veggie dishes were so delicious that I could never understand how it was my mother did not like vegetables.

My dad's dietary choices couldn't have been more different from my mother's. Not only did he embrace fruit and vegetables, but he even ate the skins of fruit that aren't designed to be eaten. Like banana peels. He still literally eats bananas without peeling them. I tried to explain that it's called the peel for a reason. My kids think this is the best party trick ever.

Our home meals brought these two conflicting perspectives about food to the table. There were a lot of Chef Boyardee ravioli dinners, as well as from-scratch mutton curries. (My parents are both Indian, and so curries were a mainstay for

dinner.) While it's not ideal to be raised on canned foods, having been exposed to these two extremes resulted in giving me a balanced perspective about how food can mean such different things to different people.

My palate became even more diverse when I was sent off to British boarding school at age seven. It was the *Oliver Twist* kind of boarding school—one where you were made to pull your socks up and were beaten (albeit gently) for crimes you never committed. Boarding school meals always had meat. A lot of meat. Meat dishes previously unfamiliar to me: steak and kidney pie, shepherd's pie, cottage pie, liver, haggis, roast lamb, lamb chops, bangers and mash, pigs in a blanket, fish and chips. There were also lots of veggies but I wasn't such a fan, as they tended to be overcooked until they were mush. Think overboiled Brussels sprouts and green beans like someone forgot they were still on the stove. (Maybe this is why I became so motivated to make veggies irresistibly delicious.) The food was so bad that we even had a rhyme about it. Sung to the tune of "Frère Jacques," it went like this:

School dinners, school dinners,
Mushy peas, mushy peas,
Soggy semolina, soggy semolina,
Doctor quick, I feel sick,
It's too late, dunnit on the plate!

Oh, and if you really, really couldn't eat something, you had to bring in a note from your parents requesting that you be excused from eating that food. You were allowed to cancel two foods—and no more. I'm assuming everyone's canceled food was some sort of vegetable, given how disgustingly they were prepared. My choices were beets and Brussels sprouts.

And then there was Montreal, where I went to college and enjoyed delicious French food. This didn't happen all too often given my limited budget as a student, but whenever I had extra money at the end of the month, I would use it to eat in some fancy French restaurant and then try to re-create those gastronomic delights in my dorm kitchen.

After graduating from college and two very short careers (if you can even call them that), one as an investment banker on Wall Street and the other as a second-grade teacher at a New York City private school, I found my way to Columbia University, where I completed a master's degree in nutrition, while I also gave birth to three kids in three and a half years. It was at this point that I became focused on raising healthy children who would love vegetables. But I wasn't confident in my cooking skills and wanted to get better at making creative food. And so, when my kids were old enough to brush their own teeth and wipe their own butts, I signed up for full-time culinary school at the Natural Gourmet Institute, where I spent six months cooking vegan and vegetarian recipes.

Armed with the skills and knowledge I needed, I was now on a mission to make tempeh, the least palatable vegan protein in my opinion, utterly delicious. I am happy to say that my now teenagers are adventurous eaters who enjoy eating plants. I have, over time, learned how to make veggies, tofu, tempeh, beans, lentils—you name it—palatable to children and adults alike, without spending hours in the kitchen, and for cheap.

It was from a want of sharing these ideas with others that I started my Instagram feed, @cookingforpeanuts. The success of this feed made me realize how many people are interested in eating this way, and so, when my friend Jonathan Safran Foer suggested I write a cookbook, I went for it.

I set out to create a cookbook filled with vegan dinners that everyone would enjoy with limited, easy-to-find ingredients. Every recipe should be inexpensive, simple, and practical. But they should also use quality ingredients and be sophisticated in their own right.

After making these recipes over and over again, you will become culinary chemists, meaning you will feel confident experimenting with ingredients you have on hand to spontaneously create your own delicious recipes. Plant-based cooking will no longer feel intimidating. Quite the opposite. It will seem ridiculously easy.

I assure you that this book is neither about trying to convince you to become vegan nor about ostracizing those of you who enjoy eating meat. It's really a guide for those who are trying to eat more plant-based meals and are looking for nonintimidating recipes that are flavorful with affordable, pantry-friendly ingredients that are used over and over again and not left to gather dust on your shelves.

I hope you enjoy making these recipes as much as I enjoyed creating them. Good luck on your plant-based journey.

Nisha

Pantry Staples

Think of this list of ingredients as you would the paint colors on an artist's palette, there to be mixed, matched, and blended in all sorts of ways to create painting after painting. Or in our case, recipe after recipe.

This list consists of essential herbs, spices, condiments, oils, plant-based proteins, and other ingredients that elevate vegan cooking, ones that are used throughout the book, over and over again, to build flavor, texture, umami (meatiness), and other desirable qualities that all yummy food should have.

You'll notice that I talk about healthy fats throughout the book. Dietary fat is a vital part of a healthful, balanced diet. It's a source of essential fatty acids, "essential" meaning the body needs them but cannot make them itself. It's also needed for the absorption of the fat-soluble vitamins A, D, E, and K, which can only be absorbed if dietary fat is present. While we need fat in our diet, not all fats are created equal. It's best to choose foods that are high in the healthy types of fat (monounsaturated and polyunsaturated) and low in the unhealthful types (saturated and trans). Healthy fats are good for your heart, brain function, and overall health. They help lower your risk of heart disease and stroke. Unhealthy fats basically do the opposite. Throughout the book, I will suggest products higher in the good types of fat.

You'll also see some talk about the essential B vitamins, especially B_{12}. There are no known plant foods that are natural sources of B_{12}. Deficiency can cause anemia and irreversible damage to the nervous system. If you follow an exclusively vegan diet, it's essential to include a reliable source of vitamin B_{12}. Fortified foods and supplements are the only proven dependable sources for vegans. Fortified foods include some vegan milk alternatives, vegan spreads, yeast extracts, and breakfast cereals. However, research shows that vegans who don't take a B_{12} supplement often have inadequate B_{12} levels, so taking a supplement is the most sure way to get your B_{12}.

For some ingredients on the following pages, you'll see brands listed in parentheses next to the ingredient. These are the brands I tend to use most, but you can use whatever is readily available in your supermarket.

Herbs, Spices & Seasonings

Herbs and spices are the backbone for so many dishes. They give flavor to the dish, and ultimately, that's what successful cooking is about—building flavor. Knowing how to use herbs and spices will give you autonomy in utilizing the ingredients you have on hand to spontaneously whip up a delicious dinner.

Let's say I have just one onion left for the week, a few cloves of garlic, one-half bag of red lentils, a carton of vegetable broth, and a couple of carrots. With a few of the spices below, I'm able to make a basic but still nourishing curry. I sauté my chopped onion and sliced carrots. Then I add my minced garlic, some curry powder, cumin, coriander, and turmeric. (You will become proficient at eyeballing the amounts.) Finally, I add my rinsed red lentils, vegetable broth, and salt. I discover that I also have a couple of nonperishables—a can of coconut milk and some canned diced tomatoes. I add these to the mix near the end of the cooking process, and violà, dinner is ready. Once you are familiar with the recipes in this book, you will be pulling off meals like this with your eyes closed!

It's best to replace dried herbs and spices every six months or so, as they lose their potency and can make your recipe taste dull or—heaven forbid—dusty.

When several seasonings are to be added back to back in a recipe, I recommend combining them in a small bowl beforehand as part of your prep. This saves you from having to perform any kitchen acrobatics, trying to get all those herbs and spices in, one by one, before your garlic burns and turns bitter.

Below is a table of herbs, spices, and seasonings that show up frequently throughout the book. I have tried to group them by chapter and so that each column represents the ones that are typically used together in a recipe. That way, you can buy the specific herbs, spices, and seasonings that are needed for

Pasta; Beans & Chili; Burgers & Patties, Stuff It, Wrap It, Top It; Comfort Food	Pasta; Comfort Food	Curry; Burgers & Patties, Stuff It, Wrap It, Top It	General Use
<ul><li>cayenne</li><li>chili powder</li><li>chipotle powder</li><li>dried oregano</li><li>garlic powder</li><li>ground cumin</li><li>paprika</li><li>smoked paprika</li></ul>	<ul><li>dried basil</li><li>dried oregano</li><li>dried rosemary</li><li>dried thyme</li></ul>	<ul><li>curry powder</li><li>garam masala</li><li>ground coriander</li><li>ground cumin</li><li>turmeric</li></ul>	<ul><li>black peppercorns in a peppermill + finely ground black pepper</li><li>crushed red pepper</li><li>garlic powder</li><li>ground mustard seed (mustard powder)</li><li>ground white pepper (sometimes used in place of black pepper for its milder flavor and neutral color)</li><li>onion powder</li><li>salt</li></ul>

your favorite recipes, which hopefully will be all of them, in which case you should buy the whole list. It's not a perfect division, as there is some overlap between recipes.

Salt

We know too much sodium is not good for us, but salt brings the flavors of a dish together. Without it, food can taste pretty bland. Just keep in mind that a little salt goes a long way, which is why I always try to buy low-sodium alternatives, like low-sodium vegetable broth, tamari, and soy sauce. This gives me more control over how much salt I'm adding. The two types of salt I use are kosher salt and iodized salt. Both have their benefits, as you'll see below. I keep both in my pantry and use kosher salt most of the time. I use iodized salt every so often to make sure I'm getting a regular dose of iodine in my diet.

Iodized salt (I like Hain Iodized Sea Salt and Morton Iodized Sea Salt) is supplemented with the mineral iodine. Many of us are not getting enough iodine from our diets. We need iodine for essential bodily processes, like healthy thyroid function. Whole grains, green beans, kale, and organic potatoes are a few iodine-rich plant-based foods, but the amount of iodine that ends up in these foods varies depending on how much is in the soil. Using a bit of iodized salt in your cooking will help you avoid becoming deficient.

Kosher salt is made of larger granules, so you can actually see how much you're adding to a dish. Plus, many chefs feel that it tastes better. It also contains about 30 percent less sodium than an equal measure of iodized salt, so you're more likely to end up with a lower sodium meal by using kosher salt. The crystal size of kosher salt varies by brand. I use Diamond Crystal kosher salt which has flatter, pyramid shaped crystals, resulting in less salt by weight than the denser, pebble shaped variety.

Oils & Fats

With my recipes, you could get away with having just one neutral-flavored cooking oil and a bottle of toasted sesame oil in your pantry. But I personally like to keep several varieties, including a bottle of extra-virgin olive oil, which I use often because of its multiple health benefits.

It used to be that we were told not to cook with extra-virgin olive oil because of its lower smoke point, or the temperature at which an oil starts to smoke. But recent studies have shown that the stability of extra-virgin olive oil is not determined by its smoke point (350°F to 410°F) but by its oxidative stability. Oxidative stability—the temperature at which the oil starts to break down and release toxic volatile compounds—is actually the best predictor of how an oil behaves at different temperatures. And it turns out that extra-virgin olive oil is oxidatively stable at the cooking-temperature ranges used in most home kitchens. (This might be because of its high levels of antioxidants.) So, if you're attached to that bottle of extra-virgin olive oil, as I am, go ahead and use it for cooking. But there is one drawback. Because it's an unrefined oil, meaning it's undergone minimal processing (which is a good thing, as fewer nutrients are destroyed, giving it additional health benefits), its distinct flavor is left intact, which makes it unsuitable for certain recipes in this book because it can throw off the intended flavor of the dish. It's for this reason you'll sometimes see a recipe call for a neutral cooking oil. These are listed on the following page, so you'll know which oils I'm referring to when you read this.

Uses

Olive Oil

Wherever you see "olive oil" in a recipe, you can use either refined olive oil (which is flavorless), extra-virgin olive oil (which tends to have a distinct flavor), or one of the other neutral-flavored cooking oils from the list below.

Extra-Virgin Olive Oil

A handful of recipes specifically calls for extra-virgin olive oil because it's the best option for that dish due to its flavor profile.

Neutral Cooking Oil

When the recipe specifically calls for a neutral cooking oil, choose one from the list below.

- **avocado, refined**
- **canola**
- **corn**
- **grapeseed**
- **olive oil (refined)**
- **safflower**
- **sesame (regular)**
- **soybean**
- **sunflower**
- **vegetable**

I recommend that you also have these oils on hand:

- **extra-virgin olive oil**

- **toasted sesame oil** (for Asian-inspired dishes)

- **vegan butter** (I like Earth Balance brand): Some recipes call for vegan butter instead of oil. This vegan alternative to butter is made from plant-based milk. It's similar in texture and mouthfeel to butter.

Note that oils should be stored in a cool, dry place and used within a year to avoid rancidity. Check for an "off" or paint-like odor before using. Read the labels for additional storage recommendations or "use by" dates.

Condiments

When a dish tastes like something is lacking, or is too acidic, or is in need of a hint of sweetness to meld the flavors together, I head for my pantry condiments. These items tend to be shelf-stable and, once opened, last for quite some time in the refrigerator. (Miso and some types of mayonnaise require refrigeration even before they are opened.) These condiments are used throughout the book, so I very much doubt they'll go to waste. With five people to feed, and a New York City apartment without a formally designated pantry space, I penny-pinch when it comes to food shopping and avoid splurging on ingredients I know I'll hardly use.

Having these handpicked condiments available will make you a more confident cook when you see how easy it is to fix a dish—especially one you think you've totally screwed up—simply by adding a condiment or two, or three, or four! Working your way through these recipes will familiarize you with which types of condiments to use based on the other ingredients in the dish.

- **chili-garlic sauce**

- **coconut aminos** (I like Bragg brand): Made from the fermented sap of a coconut palm tree and sea salt, this tastes nothing like coconut! With a salty, umami flavor, it's a gluten-free alternative to soy sauce that is usually lower in sodium and with a touch of sweetness. It can be substituted for soy sauce or tamari in a 1:1 ratio. There are many uses beyond those in this cookbook: Add it to roasted or steamed veggies, salads, veggie stir-fries, and most savory dishes.

- **Dijon mustard**

- **ketchup:** either store-bought (preferably low in sodium and added sugars) or homemade (see page 265)

- **maple syrup:** This is my preferred choice of sweetener. Pure maple syrup undergoes less processing than refined sugars. It also contains several antioxidants and minerals.

- **mellow (white) miso:** Miso, a traditional Japanese seasoning, is a fermented paste made from soybeans inoculated with a mold called koji, plus salt and rice or barley. The mellow, or white, type is milder in flavor than other varieties. With umami, salty, and earthy qualities, miso is very versatile and used throughout the book in pasta sauces, cream sauces, Asian sauces, marinades, chilis, and bean dishes. It's stored in the refrigerator and can last up to one year.

- **soy sauce (preferably low sodium)**

- **sriracha:** a hot sauce made from a paste of chili peppers, distilled vinegar, garlic, sugar, and salt

- **tamari (preferably low sodium):** This condiment is typically gluten-free, and can be used as a substitute for soy sauce, though it has a richer flavor and is less salty. If you are not gluten-free, it's ideal to keep both soy sauce and tamari, preferably low sodium, in your pantry and experiment with both to see which you prefer in various dishes.

- **Thai red curry paste** (I like Thai Kitchen and Mekhala brands)

- **vegan mayonnaise**

- **vegan Worcestershire sauce** (I like Annie's and The Wizard's brands)

All Things Tomato

These tomato-based ingredients are available in both cans and glass jars. Either is fine. I tend to prefer jars, as they can be stored as is directly in the refrigerator once they are opened, and the finished jars can be recycled into other uses, such as displaying my kid's pebble collection!

Both cans and jars are shelf-stable and last a really long time. Once opened, transfer any remaining canned tomatoes or tomato paste to a tightly covered plastic container or glass jar, and use within seven days of opening.

- **diced tomatoes**

- **fire-roasted tomatoes:** These tomatoes are richer in flavor than regular diced tomatoes. They are charred over a flame before being diced, giving them a fierce and fiery quality. I tend to use them in chilis, curries, soups, and tomato-based pasta sauces.

- **tomato paste**

Vinegars

Vinegars are an essential ingredient in cooking. They are used to brighten and balance a dish.

You don't want to overuse them, or your dish will become too acidic. But when used in the right amounts, they help bring the dish together.

Rice vinegar is mostly used in Asian dishes or marinades. The other vinegars in the list are used extensively in cooking to make salad dressings, for flavoring marinades, to drizzle on low-moisture veggies fresh out of the oven, or even to make vegan buttermilk, which is pretty

neat. (Note: If you're using vinegar for a salad dressing, the optimal ratio is about 4 parts oil to 1 part vinegar.) My point is, your vinegars won't go to waste, especially if you use them in creative ways beyond the recipes in this book. I have suggested four vinegars that I like to use, but you can get by with just two and some fresh lemon juice.

While vinegars don't expire as such, they tend to lose their oomph after six months to a year. To help keep them fresh, store in a cool, dark place with the lid tightly closed.

Now, while this book's focus is budget-friendly cooking, it's worth investing in high-quality balsamic and red wine vinegars, otherwise you may decide to use them for cleaning the lime scale in your kettle! (Yes, vinegars are good for that, too, but cheap white vinegar is best for this purpose.)

- **apple cider vinegar**

- **balsamic vinegar** (optional)

- **red wine vinegar** (or substitute apple cider vinegar or lemon juice)

- **rice vinegar**

Other Shelf-Stable Essentials

- **Nutritional yeast** (I like the Bragg brand): Also known as "nooch," this adds a cheesy, nutty flavor to foods. It's used most often for seasoning pasta dishes, veggies, and salads, but it's good sprinkled on popcorn, in place of Parmesan cheese, for vegan cheese sauce, stirred into soups for added nutrients and flavor, and in tofu scrambled eggs.

  Nutritional yeast is similar to the yeast used in baking, but it's been heated and dried, rendering it inactive, so it won't make your pasta sauce rise!

  It's dairy-free, usually gluten-free, and surprisingly high in protein, containing all nine essential amino acids, which makes it a complete protein. Fortified brands are a good source of B vitamins, including B_{12}, which is nonexistent in exclusively vegan diets (except in supplemented foods). Not all varieties of nutritional yeast sold are fortified with B_{12}, so be sure to check your product's label for its nutritional content. In some brands, the B vitamin levels can be much higher than the required amounts, so use sparingly.

- **Unsweetened canned coconut milk** (I like Thai Kitchen brand): Not to be confused with the kind that comes in a carton, which is for cereals and smoothies, canned coconut milk lends body, flavor, and richness to a dish. Regular coconut milk does a better job of this, but the lite version (made with less fat) will also work.

- **Unsweetened nondairy milk:** My preference is soy milk, because it has a thicker consistency from all the healthy fats and it's fortified with B_{12}. Almond milk and most other nondairy milks are fine to use, too. Some of these other nondairy milks may also be fortified with B_{12}, but less consistently than soy milk, so make sure to read the nutrition label if that's a concern.

  If you don't consume nondairy milk on a regular basis, for example in smoothies, cereals, or for drinking, you can buy the ultra-high temperature (UHT) processed type, which is shelf-stable until opened or until the expiration date.

- **Vegetable broth** (I like low-sodium Pacific Foods and Imagine brands): Resealable, twist-open cartons are my preferred choice as any remaining broth can easily be stored in the refrigerator.

Nuts & Seeds

I'm nuts about nuts, but I know there are a lot of folks with nut and seed allergies who can't afford to be nuts about nuts (or seeds). For this reason, I've tried not to include too many nutty recipes in this book. Generally, the cashew cream, tahini, and nut butter recipes are best left as written, but peanuts, sesame seeds, and pumpkin seeds that are used as garnishes can easily be omitted.

Incorporating nuts into a recipe is a convenient way of adding protein, fiber, and healthy fats into our diet. They have the potential to transform a simple recipe into a more substantial and satisfying meal. They also have massive amounts of minerals, as well as phytonutrients that support those good gut bacteria you're always hearing about. I find it fascinating that a healthy gut makes for a healthy brain.

Additionally, nuts have incredibly versatile textures. Chopped nuts will add a crunch to your burgers, and nut butters will make your sauce deliciously creamy.

- **cashews (unsalted, raw, not roasted):** These are the gold standard in making vegan dishes creamy. They're used in sauces, curries, dips, and dressings. They do need to be soaked before blending, which requires some planning ahead, or they won't blend smoothly. Either soak them overnight with enough water to cover or do a quick soak in hot water for at least an hour before blending. If you own a powerful high-speed blender, like a Vitamix, you likely won't need to soak your cashews at all.

- **nut butter, peanut or almond (smooth):** used for thickening sauces and giving them a creamy texture

- **peanuts:** Do you know that peanuts are actually legumes? Yet they have the audacity to use "nut" in their name! So cheeky!

- **pumpkin seeds (unsalted):** Lightly toasting your seeds makes them even more flavorful and deliciously crunchier, but it's not required. These versatile seeds have many uses beyond the recipes in this book. Add them to salads, creamy pasta dishes, roasted veggies, creamy soups, pesto, and patties.

- **sesame seeds:** They may be tiny, but sesame seeds pack a good amount of calcium and iron, both of which can be a bit low in vegan diets. They also add a delicious sesame flavor, which is enhanced by lightly toasting them before using. For the recipes in this book, they are mostly used as a garnish for the Asian Fake-Out dishes in chapter 5.

- **tahini:** This smooth paste is made from ground sesame seeds. It's useful for thickening sauces and making them creamier, plus it adds a good amount of protein to a dish. I use it in curries, chilis, sauces, dips, and dressings. This is one of my all-time favorite ingredients. My kids think they hate tahini, yet they can't even tell that it's in so many of their favorite dishes! *Shhh!*

Dry Ingredients

- **baking soda:** Used in some pasta sauces to neutralize the acid from the tomatoes, baking soda should be stored in the refrigerator to absorb any bad odors; replace it at least every three months.

- **cornstarch:** used to thicken sauces and batters, or for coating tofu to make it extra crispy

- **dried bread crumbs and panko bread crumbs**

- **flax meal (ground flaxseeds):** Pack in those omega-3s by adding some to hot or cold cereal, oatmeal, or yogurt. Or stir some into soups, chilis, and sauces as a thickener. Add some to your mayonnaise or mustard when making a sandwich, or bake it into cookies, muffins, and breads. Flax meal is often used as a replacement for chicken eggs in vegan recipes and is called a flax egg.

To make one flax egg, simply combine 1 tablespoon flax meal with 2½ tablespoons water and set aside for at least 10 minutes. Sometimes I refrigerate the mixture if I want the "egg" to be a gooier consistency. Or I might add more water for a thinner consistency depending on the recipe.

- **whole-wheat pastry flour or all-purpose flour**

those in this book include as a low-sodium salt alternative; for sprinkling on popcorn, salads, and sandwiches; and for adding to dressings. I usually stick with dulse granules for my recipes, because some types of seaweed, specifically kombu, can have dangerously high levels of iodine, which can be detrimental to the thyroid.

- **gochujang:** Savory, sweet, and spicy, this Korean red chili paste is used in marinades and dipping sauces, or to add a punch to soups or stews.

- **kala namak (Himalayan or Indian black salt):** A salt with a savory umami flavor reminiscent of hard-boiled eggs, kala namak is used in vegan cooking to give a dish an eggy flavor. Like eggs, it contains sulfur, which is what gives it that distinctive taste and smell. (The smell is also reminiscent of farts, but fear not, it dissipates upon cooking!)

More Ingredients to Elevate Your Plant-Based Cooking

These ingredients are not technically essential, because the recipes work perfectly well without them. But they will take your dish to the next level and bring out its maximum potential. They're fun ingredients to play with, and I highly recommend keeping them around.

- **dark soy sauce:** This type is aged longer than regular soy sauce, making it richer, thicker, and darker in color. It is used for adding color and more flavor to Asian dishes.

- **dulse flakes or granules:** This is essentially dried seaweed and an excellent source of iodine, a mineral often lacking in our diets. Dulse granules are used in vegan dishes to add a sealike quality by mimicking the scent and taste of seafood. Other uses beyond

Other Nonperishables

On the following page is a list of other staples I keep in my pantry that are geared towards the recipes I make most often. You will ultimately end up with your own list, based on the recipes that tend to interest you. For more perishable items, like veggies, avocados, and fresh herbs, I prefer to purchase these at the start of each week for the recipes I know I'm going to be making.

Legumes
(Beans & Lentils)

Beans, beans,
Good for your heart.
The more you eat,
The more you fart.
The more you fart,
The better you feel,
So let's eat beans,
With every meal.

I know, beans can make you gassy, which is why many people avoid eating them. Believe me, with five bean eaters living like sardines in a New York City apartment, I get it! There are ways to help alleviate this unpleasant side effect: Incorporate beans gradually into your diet, soak dried beans before use and rinse them well, eat beans more often so your body gets better at digesting them, and chew and savor your beans. Scoffing them down can also cause more gas.

Legumes are so incredibly healthy that they're worth a little wind. They are not only a low-calorie source of protein but also high in fiber, which keeps us regular and appears to protect against heart disease, high blood pressure, and digestive illness.

Below is a list of the legumes I keep in my pantry. These show up regularly in the recipes in this book. (See page 38 for equivalents and soaking tips.)

Canned or Dried Beans
- black beans
- chickpeas (garbanzos)
- kidney beans
- pinto beans

Dried Lentils
- brown lentils
- green lentils
- red lentils

Grains

Grains are good sources of complex carbohydrates (fiber and starch), as well as key vitamins and minerals. It's best to choose whole grains over refined grains whenever possible. Whole grains are naturally high in fiber, which lets us feel full and satisfied, so we're less likely to overeat, making it easier to maintain a healthy body weight. Whole grains are also linked to a decreased risk of heart disease, diabetes, and certain cancers. There are other benefits, too, like a healthy colon. (Sorry to keep bringing up colons, but I remain traumatized by my mother's invasive colectomy!)

Refined grains have been milled to remove the bran and germ (parts of their seed), giving them a finer texture and longer shelf life. The downside is that the refining process removes many nutrients, including fiber. That's part of the reason why it takes so many slices of Wonder Bread to make you feel full!

Having said that, it's not going to end the universe if you have a big bowl of white rice with your curry once in a while or your favorite white pasta shape (mine is radiatori) with your tofu Bolognese. (Many of the cooler pasta shapes don't come in whole-grain varieties.) After all, life is about balance and having some creature comforts.

Some of the whole-grain choices pertaining to the recipes in this book include millet and buckwheat ramen noodles, buckwheat mushroom ramen noodles, buckwheat soba noodles, brown rice noodles, whole-wheat pasta, brown rice, and quinoa, which is not technically a grain but included here. (I like the Lotus Foods brand for my noodles.)

Below is a list of grains that show up throughout the book, but there are many other wholesome and versatile whole grains that can be used in place of these, such as farro, barley, bulgur wheat, and millet.

- noodles: ramen, rice, udon (wheat)
- pasta
- quinoa
- rice

The Essential Aromatics

Yellow onions, garlic, and ginger are used in recipe after recipe throughout this book. They impart deep flavors and release addictive aromas. They also have a lot of health benefits.

Partly because they're used so extensively around the globe, onions are among the most significant sources of antioxidants in the human diet. They also contain a particularly valuable flavonoid, quercetin, which acts as an antioxidant and has been linked to preventing cancer. Garlic is thought to be helpful in lowering blood pressure and cholesterol, reducing the risk of cancer, and strengthening the immune system. It's also believed to have significant anti-inflammatory properties. Ginger is known to have anti-inflammatory, antibacterial, and antiviral qualities. In short, use these aromatics as much as possible to flavor your dishes. They're healthy, delicious, and relatively inexpensive.

There's nothing wrong with buying pre-chopped or pre-peeled aromatics or veggies. Peeled garlic, diced onion, cubed butternut squash, chopped sweet potato, you name it—if it makes your life easier and it's available in your supermarket, don't feel like a cop-out for going that route. Making a home-cooked meal is already a huge achievement. No brownie points lost for not doing the chopping! Alternatively, you can use a mini food chopper (I like Ninja brand) to quickly cut up your aromatics.

Below are some tips for keeping your garlic, ginger, and onions fresh. Store them properly, and they will last a good while.

Garlic

Store at room temperature in a dry, dark, and well-ventilated room or cabinet. Use a mesh bag or basket, or no container at all, for storing. Once you break a bulb (a garlic one, that is), use the remaining cloves within ten days.

Ginger Root

Store in a freezer bag or brown paper bag in the crisper drawer of your refrigerator. It should keep for about a week.

Onions

Store in a cool, dry, dark, and well-ventilated room or cabinet. Use a mesh bag or a box with holes to hold your onions. They can be stored this way for about a month.

Frozen Veggies

These veggies arrive fresh, at peak ripeness, to the processing plant. Because of this, frozen veggies are sometimes even more nutritious than their fresh counterparts you find in the supermarket. So don't fall for the misconception that you lose nutrients when you freeze produce. Fresh and frozen veggies are generally nutritionally equal to one another. And the frozen ones have the added advantage of sitting in your freezer at your beck and call!

Conveniently, most of the recipes here that use frozen veggies don't require that you thaw them beforehand.

- **green peas**
- **riced cauliflower**
- **sweet corn**

Tofu & Tempeh

I like to keep at least one package of each of these in my refrigerator at all times. They are both excellent sources of plant-based protein, calcium, and iron. Some brands have more than others, however, so it's important to check the nutrition labels.

Tofu is made from condensed, unfermented soy milk that's been processed into solid blocks. It's generally flavorless, which is an excellent thing for us culinary chemists, as it easily takes on the flavor of marinades and sauces. All except one of the tofu recipes in this book calls for extra-firm tofu; it holds its shape well and is easy to slice and cube. This is the best choice for pan-frying, stir-frying, baking, grilling, crumbling, and scrambling. Silken tofu also makes an appearance as a base for a nut-free, creamy sauce. This type of tofu works well in smooth and blended foods, like salad dressings, sauces, and dips.

Tofu is typically sold in a plastic container filled with water to keep it fresh. This excess liquid should be drained by pressing the tofu for about twenty minutes before use, or the tofu will steam instead of crisping up and will end up flavorless. There is a way to avoid this time-consuming process: Scour the tofu section in your supermarket and look for "super-firm" or "sprouted" tofu, which has been prepressed for you. Nasoya super-firm tofu and Wildwood extra-firm sprouted tofu are two brands I have used, and they have been a godsend for getting dinner on the table at lightning speed. Plus, because they are denser, they are quite a bit higher in protein than other extra-firm tofu.

Tempeh is very different from tofu, even though they are both made from soybeans. It has an earthy, nutty quality and is quite a bit higher in protein. It's often sold as an alternative to meat. Think "tempeh bacon." It's made by fermenting partially cooked soybeans with a beneficial type of mold (rhizopus). In this case, mold is a good thing! It adds nutrients to the tempeh and makes it easier to digest, which translates into no bloating or gas, making it the perfect first-date food! People either love it or hate it, but I'm convinced that if you make the tempeh recipes in this book, you (and your date) will become lovers of tempeh indefinitely.

I know there's conflicting information out there about consuming soy, specifically tofu, and many people question whether it's safe and healthy to eat. Soy has a lot of health benefits and serves as an excellent protein source in plant-based diets. Regarding its safety, recent evidence-based studies do not point to any dangers to humans from eating soy. The estrogen-like compounds (phytoestrogens) in soy have not been found to increase the risk of breast cancer. In fact, there is growing evidence that soy foods, like tofu and tempeh, may lower the risk of breast cancer because the phytoestrogens may actually block the potent natural estrogens in the blood. And rest assured, the estrogen-like compounds in soy are not going to act like regular estrogen and start producing undesirable changes that you would expect from hormones. My husband has been eating soy for years—soy milk, tofu, and tempeh—and he still hasn't grown any breasts! I would know!!!

Types

- **tempeh** (I like Lightlife and Trader Joe's brands)

- **tofu: extra-firm, super-firm, or extra-firm/ sprouted** (I like Wildwood and Nasoya brands)

Kitchen Essentials

Invest in These Basics

I'm a minimalist at heart. I generally don't buy something unless its value trumps the real-estate cost of storing it in my NYC apartment, which already houses three kids, a husband, and all the junk they've hoarded over the years. My bohemian-esque youngest daughter has two hand-me-down sewing machines she never uses, a typewriter she never uses, a label maker she never uses, a most extravagant baking decoration kit she never uses, and enough yarn to wrap around the globe a few times over!

This is not how I roll. My kitchen is curated with cookware and appliances that have proven to be worth their weight in gold when it comes to convenience and practicality. For me, these essentials have made cooking even more enjoyable and have cut down on the time it takes to get dinner on the table. They make the cooking process go much more smoothly, allowing me to get more creative in the kitchen. You don't need all of these items to make the recipes in this book; your essentials will be based on the recipes you choose to cook and how often you make them. That being said, all of these items are used over and over again in my kitchen, and you won't regret having them.

Blender

You certainly don't have to fork over $400 for a Vitamix to successfully make these recipes, but if you are able to, it's well worth it. It cuts out having to soak nuts for making creamy sauces or homemade nut butters, and is a monster when it comes to getting things really smooth.

When shopping for a blender, you'll notice there are regular blenders and then there are high-speed blenders. If you're the saucy type, meaning you're into making smooth sauces, dressings, creamy soups, and the like, I would invest in a high-speed blender. These are more powerful and have better designed blades. If you decide to go with a high-speed one, there's the Vitamix, but there are other brands with solid options, including Wolf, Breville, Ninja, and Blendtec. I would do some research and see which ones have the best reviews and are in your price range. Choose the best-quality one you can afford.

Immersion Blender

Like the name implies, this type of blender literally gets immersed in your sauce, soup, or curry. Right there in the pot. No need to transfer all that messy stuff to a blender. But if you're okay with transferring the messy stuff, there's no need to purchase one of these.

Food Processor

Contrary to its name, this does not make processed food! Like a blender, a food processor has blades. But these blades are designed differently. They are made to achieve the right consistency for pesto, hummus, guacamole, patties, and falafels, to name a few, without turning them into smoothies. A food processor incorporates all the ingredients you have so conveniently tossed inside and gives you the control over how creamy or textured you want the end product to be. It also serves as a food and vegetable chopper, which significantly cuts down on prep time.

Don't make the mistake of using your blender as a food processor, or vice versa. You may end up with a falafel smoothie or banana blueberry hummus!

Chef's Knife (8- or 10-Inch)

You have two options here. Option one is to think of this purchase as you might pick out your soul mate: You want them to be there for you through thick and thin (literally). If this is your thinking, research the most highly reviewed chef's knives on the market and buy the best one you can afford. A good-quality chef's knife will last you a lifetime, and it's the tool you will use most often in the kitchen. If you do go this route, you will also need a couple of smaller knives, including a serrated utility knife (helpful for slicing tomatoes) and a paring knife for cutting smaller items (like garlic cloves). These don't need to be anything fancy. They just need to get the job done.

Option two is to think of this purchase as a one-night stand. (Though it will last you much longer

than one night, maybe even a couple of years, depending on how often you use them and how you care for them.) You buy a cheap knife set, use them until they've seen their day, and then replace them with a new set. This isn't good for the environment, and you're sacrificing on quality, but it's another option if this is what you can afford or if you're not going to get your "real deal" chef's knife sharpened at least twice a year. If this is the route you're going to take, I recommend the Cuisinart twelve-piece knife set with blade guards for about $20. I know a lot of people who have these and are very happy with them.

Now here's the deal with keeping those knives sharp. Contrary to what you might think, dull knives are way more dangerous than sharp knives—in the kitchen at least! You'll know you need to get your knife sharpened when you're struggling to cut through that tomato.

If you go with the real-deal chef's knife, you should get it professionally sharpened at least twice a year. It'll cost you less than $10 and is worth every penny. Sharpening your own knives properly is a skill in itself, one I still haven't mastered. I do sharpen my chef's knife once in a while, but not the way I was taught in culinary school. (Oops! Did I just say that?) I cheat with the MinoSharp 3 Sharpener. It does a reasonable job and is very easy to use, but it's quite pricey. I use this in between having my knife professionally sharpened.

If you want cheaper, mediocre knife sets to last longer, you will need to buy some sort of home sharpener. Research the best ones in your budget.

Keep your knives sharp, friends.

Cutting Board

Ideally, you want to get yourself a large, heavy-duty cutting board that won't move around while you're trying to chop those onions and bawling your eyes out. (I always have a good cry when I chop onions!) You're less likely to cut yourself, and your diced onions won't end up all over the countertop. It's also worth having a smaller one for when there's not much to chop. (Don't you love those dinners?) Wooden cutting boards harbor less bacteria than plastic, they're pretty solid so they won't move around as much, and they'll keep your knives sharper for longer. High-quality wood would be my preference (teak, maple, walnut), but it can be pricey.

There is a more budget-friendly option that works well enough. I recently purchased an OXO Good Grips Utility Cutting Board because I wanted something more lightweight for the kids. It's made from nonporous thermoplastic, which doesn't retain odors (in other words, it doesn't get stinky), and it doesn't appear to be dulling my knives either. Plus, it has nonslip edges that keep it in place.

Nonstick Skillet with Lid (Cast Iron, Ceramic, Stone-Derived, or Other Nonstick Finish)

You will use less oil with these types of skillets, plus cooking in them is really easy. Getting your tofu to brown, your sweet potatoes to caramelize, and your chickpeas to turn crunchy, all without clinging to the pan, is a breeze with a nonstick surface. I highly recommend investing in at least two different sizes: 10-inch and 12-inch. Stick with the healthier types of nonstick when possible, like the ones I have mentioned.

Cast-iron cookware is reasonably priced and very durable. And because it's made from iron, cooking with it gets more iron into your diet. Makes sense, right? But it does require more maintenance than other types of nonstick cookware. To prevent rusting and to preserve its nonstick quality, cast iron should be washed using hot water and a metal mesh scrub or bristle brush; wipe dry with a cloth kitchen towel and place it over the burner on low to evaporate any remaining moisture. A thin layer of cooking oil should then be applied all over with a paper towel before storing the pan.

I own all three types of skillets, but my go-to is the Ozeri Stone Earth Frying Pan. It looks a bit like the ceramic ones, but it uses a nontoxic, nonstick stone-derived coating from Germany. It

works amazingly well, and its nonstick quality is the same as the day I bought it, which is about two years ago. I have the 10- and 12-inch frying pans. The only care required is that you wait until they cool before washing them, and use either plastic, wooden, or silicone cooking utensils.

2-Quart & 4-Quart Saucepans with Lids

For pastas, grains, sauces, curries, chilis—you name it, they've got you covered.

Large Sauté Pan with Lid

In reality, you could get by with your large skillet and lid, but sauté pans are incredibly convenient to have around. They're not just for sautéing, unlike the name implies. They have many different uses because of their unique shape.

Sauté pans have straight sides that are taller than a skillet's, making them a good choice for cooking liquid recipes such as curries, stews, and sauces, as well as for frying, braising, boiling, and—let's not forget—sautéing. I also use them for cooking spaghetti and one-pot pastas. Nonstick is preferable, as it works better for one-pot pasta dinners.

Cooking Utensils

A seemingly easy purchase, but in actuality, choosing the right utensils is more complicated than you might think. The ideal utensils are nontoxic, won't scratch your pan, and won't melt in it either. Plastic-crusted tofu doesn't taste all that great. I've tried it!

The most practical and durable I have found are those made from high-heat-resistant silicone that are safe to at least 400°F. Beware: Some utensils are sold as high-heat silicone but have plastic handles. This is problematic when you rest that spatula on the side of the pan to go grab a sip of coffee or a swig of wine—and upon your return, you find that your pan is now coated in melted plastic. I learned this the hard way. So, it's worth your while to buy good-quality solid silicone utensils.

My recommendation is to purchase a couple of larger silicone spoons for stirring, mixing, and serving (wooden spoons would also work if you already own these); two silicone spatulas (large and small); two pairs of tongs (large and small) with scalloped silicone edges for turning hot foods on a baking sheet or in a pan; and a silicone ladle for soupy stuff.

I also own a heavy-duty metal spoon and a perforated spoon that I use in my regular saucepans. Stainless steel works well for your *not* nonstick cookware.

Rimmed Baking Sheets

For patties, veggies, potatoes eight ways (except for mashed), sweet potato fries, and all that good stuff that goes in the oven, you definitely need a baking sheet or two. And seeing as some recipes require a rimmed baking sheet, you might as well purchase the rimmed ones (large and small) for all your baking or roasting needs in this book. Make your life easier and go with the nonstick type. I also own silicone baking mats that can be used to line any type of baking sheet. They're very handy. They don't retain flavors and are heat resistant up to about 480°F. They can be used over and over again and are easy to clean. Parchment paper can also be used for lining baking sheets. The negatives of parchment are that it's not environmentally friendly, as you have to throw it out after most uses, and it tends to sometimes steam the food and not get it quite as crispy as using a silicone mat. But both work well for these recipes, so it's your call.

Dry Measuring Cups & Spoons

If you already own a complete set of each, go ahead and use what you have. But if you're in the market for a new set, I do have some strong opinions about this seemingly mundane purchase, the first being that it's not as mundane as you might think. You spend a lot of time with your cups and spoons. They show up in almost every recipe and are quite impactful on your culinary experience. It's worth putting some thought into them.

Not all sets are created equal. Some come with more sizes, and some with less. Make your life easier and go with a set that gives you a wider range of options so you can measure accurately.

For measuring spoons, purchase a set that includes both ¾-teaspoon and ⅛-teaspoon measurements. Also note the shape of the spoon. Round spoons are a major pet peeve of mine. You literally have to pour your spices and herbs directly into the spoon because they don't fit into most spice jars. It's a hit-or-miss situation. My life took a turn for the better when I discovered there were rectangular measuring spoons, designed to fit into spice jars. How did I miss this? I didn't realize how poorly designed the round ones were until I found the rectangular ones. I remain confused as to why round spoons were made in the first place, or why spice jars didn't account for the size of spoons. It's a chicken-and-egg situation. Which came first? The spice jar or the measuring spoon?

As for measuring cups, I recommend purchasing a set that includes ⅔-, ¾-, and 2-cup measurements. But don't get your knickers in a twist if you can't find such a set.

Finally, try to avoid plastic sets if possible. They're bulkier and become a bit toxic at high temperatures. Go with stainless steel if you can. I own the fifteen-piece Hudson Essentials stainless-steel measuring cups and spoons. It's one of the best cooking investments I've made. There are comparable sets available on Amazon that are less pricey.

Microplane Grater-Zester

You'll need one of these for grating ginger, garlic, and lemon and lime zests.

Other Items

Whisk, peeler, potato masher, nesting mixing bowls, liquid measuring cup, colander, fine-mesh strainer, and a steaming basket or steamer

Techniques & Tips

Culinary Tricks You'll Want to Know

Tofu

Pressing Tofu

You may see "press tofu" in a recipe and wonder, "What the heck does that mean?" Let me explain. Pressing tofu is literally that: pressing the block of tofu. We do this to remove excess water so the tofu is easier to work with. We don't want our tofu falling apart. That would be a culinary nightmare. We want it firm in texture and as dry as humanly possible so it is easier to cut, soaks up the marinade, and turns a beautiful golden brown when we bake or sauté it.

Three Ways to Get the Job Done

- **Let someone else do the pressing for you and save yourself twenty minutes.** Prepressed tofu is becoming more widely available in supermarkets and health food stores.

Look for the words *super firm or extra-firm sprouted* on the package. I've used Nasoya super-firm tofu and Wildwood extra-firm sprouted tofu, and they're game-changers when you're in a rush to get dinner on the table, which is basically every night!

- **Buy a tofu press.** This is a small contraption that will press your tofu for you. I have the Tofuture tofu press, and it's very easy to use and clean. You will still need to press your tofu for at least twenty minutes, but you can plan ahead and do it the night before, leave the contraption in your refrigerator, and you're all ready to go come dinnertime.

- **Use a heavy object.** Remove the block of tofu from its packaging. Fold a few paper towels in half and place them on a cutting board. Place the block of tofu on top of the folded paper towels. Place a few more folded paper towels on top of the block of tofu. Place a smaller cutting board on top of the top layer of paper towels. Set a bowl on top and fill it with heavy produce, like apples, onions, oranges, or a large cauliflower—you get the picture. (If the paper towels become very wet, replace them.) Do not apply too

Just try to get them as equal in size as you can for even cooking.

Cubes

- Turn the block of tofu on its side, with the longer side faceup. Slice it lengthwise down the middle.

- Keeping the block intact, flip it over to lie flat on the cutting board.

- Slice lengthwise down the middle, so that you have 2 even halves. (Total of 4 pieces: 2 on top, 2 underneath)

- Slice each half in half, lengthwise, so that you have 4 equal rectangles. (Total of 8 pieces: 4 on top, 4 underneath)

- Make 3 equally spaced cuts, widthwise, for a total of 16 cubes on top. You now have 32 equal-sized cubes: 16 on top, 16 underneath.

Rectangles

- Lay the block of tofu flat on the cutting board.

- Slice it widthwise down the middle, so that you have 2 even halves. (Total number of pieces: 2)

- Slice each half in half, widthwise. (Total number of pieces: 4)

- For 8 rectangles: Slice each quarter in half, widthwise, so that you have 8 equal-sized rectangles. (Total number of pieces: 8)

- For 12 rectangles: Slice each quarter into thirds, widthwise, so that you have 12 equal-sized rectangles. (Total number of pieces: 12)

Triangles

- Follow the steps above for making rectangles. (Total number of rectangles: 8)

- Lay the rectangles flat on the cutting board. Slice each one diagonally into 2 long triangles, making 16 equal-sized triangles.

Cutlets

- Turn the block of tofu onto its side, with the longer side faceup.

much weight or your tofu will be crushed. And you'll be crushed, too, at having to start dinner all over again.

Freezing Your Tofu

Now why on earth would we be freezing tofu overnight, only to spend time defrosting it to its unfrozen state again? This seemingly time-wasting process is actually extremely valuable. It gives the tofu a chewy texture that deliciously mimics chicken. In fact, if you repeat this process twice—freeze, defrost, freeze, defrost—it's even more yummy.

When a recipe calls for you to freeze the tofu, you can do so in its original packaging.

Cutting Your Pressed Tofu

If you totally botch up these shapes, don't sweat it. You can still make the dish with whatever shape or shapes you end up with.

Tofu cutting

- Slice through the long side lengthwise three times to make 3 equal-sized slabs (large rectangles).

Tempeh

Prepping Your Tempeh

If tempeh isn't yet your thing, or if you haven't tried it, I'm convinced that my little tricks will turn you into a fan. After all, I now have three tempeh-loving girls, remember?

Tempeh does tend to have an aftertaste that a lot of people don't like. I have a foolproof method for turning that around and giving it a delicious aftertaste. I briefly simmer the block of tempeh before using it in a recipe. This removes the bitterness associated with tempeh and opens up its pores so it can more readily absorb the flavorful seasonings. In some of my recipes, I go a step further and crumble the tempeh before seasoning it. Then I bake

it, giving it a slightly crispy texture. Only then do we add our sauce. You won't taste any unpleasantness once you've put your tempeh through this wringer! Who says tempeh has to be an acquired taste? Let's make it yummy to begin with!

Simmering Your Tempeh Before Using (Optional, but Highly Recommended)

In a medium saucepan, bring enough water to cover the block of tempeh by about 2 inches to a boil. Add the tempeh, reduce the heat, and simmer for 3 minutes. Drain the tempeh and pat it dry. Set aside to cool before cutting.

Cutting Your Tempeh into Rectangles

- Slice the tempeh widthwise through the middle into 2 even halves.

- Slice each half in half, making 4 even rectangular slabs.

- Place one of the rectangular slabs on its side, with the longest side faceup, and slice through the middle lengthwise, making 2 thin rectangles. (Total number of pieces: 5)

- Repeat for the remaining three slabs. You should end up with 8 thin rectangles.

(If you like your tempeh extra crispy, you can slice the rectangular slabs into 3 thin rectangles instead of 2, for a total of 12 thin rectangles. Thinner rectangles are best for making tempeh bacon.)

Mimicking Ground Meat with Tofu & Tempeh
I did eat meat growing up, so I know the texture ground meat gives to a good Bolognese or chili. After several attempts, I believe I have achieved the most delicious vegan alternative. It's the same process for both tempeh and extra-firm tofu, except with tempeh, you simmer it first (see opposite page).

Tempeh cutting

Use your hands to break up the simmered and dried tempeh or the pressed tofu into small crumbles. Do this over a large bowl to avoid spillage. Add your spices and oil to the crumbles and incorporate the ingredients using your hands, so that all those little suckers are covered. Transfer the crumbles to a nonstick rimmed baking sheet and bake at 400°F for about 15 minutes, or until golden brown and slightly crispy. Give them a good shake after 10 minutes so they cook evenly.

Alternatively, in a large nonstick skillet, sauté the crumbles in batches over medium heat for about 7 minutes, or until golden brown and slightly crispy.

Stir-Fry Basics

One of the easiest, quickest, and most delicious ways to use up your veggies and aromatics before they go bad is to make a stir-fry. At the end of this cookbook is a large assortment of stir-fry sauces you can whip up using your pantry condiments.

Below are some basics that will change your stir-fry game forever. It's taken me many stir-fry failures to develop this list that I have now committed to memory.

Do

- Prep all your ingredients before you begin. Stir-fries cook very quickly so you won't have time to do any dicing or slicing once you have food in the pan.

- Cut all of your ingredients into similarly sized pieces so they cook evenly.

- Prepare your rice or noodles before you start your stir-fry.

- The oil should be hot before you add your ingredients. We want your protein and veggies to sizzle. Test first with one piece.

- Cook in batches if necessary. Don't overcrowd the pan or your protein and veggies will steam instead of becoming crispy.

- Stir, then fry. Then stir. Then fry. If you keep stirring the entire time, your protein and veggies will never brown.

The Steps

- Cook your protein (tofu or tempeh) first, if you plan on adding any to your stir-fry.

- Remove your protein from the wok or skillet before adding your veggies.

- Cook firmer veggies first, as they require a longer cooking time.

- Don't overcook your veggies. They should be tender-crisp.

- Push your veggies to the side of the skillet or wok once they are done cooking and add your aromatics (garlic and ginger) to the center. Cook for about 30 seconds more, or until fragrant, stirring constantly.

- Add your sauce and cooked protein to the veggies and continue cooking until the sauce starts to thicken and is warmed through.

- Serve with rice or noodles.

Beans

Easy, forgiving, healthy, and affordable! You got to love those beans.

Canned or Dried?

There's nothing wrong with using canned beans. They're convenient and keep for a long time. Remember, our first priority here is getting a plant-based dinner on the table with as little sweat as possible, and if this means using canned beans, go for it. I will say though, in the long run, cooking your own beans is more economical, and they taste better. But it requires some planning ahead, and some basic math, which I'm going to do for you.

By planning ahead, I mean soaking your beans. It's always best to soak dried beans before cooking. This helps them cook faster and more evenly, and it can also make them easier to digest, which means less flatulence. (Adding some salt to your soaking water breaks down their skins so they cook even faster.)

Soaking Your Beans

Overnight Soak

- Cover your beans with water by 2 inches. (Optional: Add 1 tablespoon fine salt per pound of beans.) Let them soak for at least 4 hours and up to 12 hours. Drain and rinse.

Quick Soak

- If you forget to soak your beans overnight, as I often do, this method also gets the job done.

- Place the beans in a saucepan. Cover with water by about 2 inches. Bring to a gentle boil. Turn off the heat, give them a good stir, and let them soak for about an hour. Drain and rinse.

Don't Soak

- Yes, you can just cook your beans without soaking. But be prepared to cook for an hour or two beyond the usual cooking time. My advice is, if you forget to soak your beans and it's time to make dinner, reach for those canned beans. I always keep some in my pantry as a backup.

Cooking Your Beans

Place your beans in a saucepan and cover them with at least 2 inches of water or veggie broth. Bring the liquid to a simmer and cook your beans until they are tender and cooked through, stirring occasionally and adding more liquid as needed. Soaked beans take anywhere from 45 minutes to 2 hours to cook. (Don't boil your beans as it can cause them to burst.)

Remember to save that cooking liquid. It's like liquid gold! Either use it in the recipe, if it calls for it, or refrigerate or freeze it to use later in a soup or chili.

Bean Equivalents

- 1 cup dried beans = 2½ to 3 cups cooked beans
- One 15-ounce can of beans, drained, is about 1½ cups cooked beans.
- A heaping ½ cup dried beans, once cooked and drained, will yield about 1½ cups cooked beans.

So, for a recipe that calls for one 15-ounce can of beans, you should cook about ½ heaping cup dried beans. I always cook more than the recipe calls for and refrigerate the remainder to use over the next 3 to 5 days.

Cooking Liquid

- One 15-ounce can of beans contains about ½ cup liquid.

So, if a recipe calls for one 15-ounce can of beans with liquid (undrained), add ½ cup of your bean cooking liquid along with your 1½ cups cooked beans.

Lentils

Dried lentils tend to be foamy when added to water because of the soapy-tasting saponins in their skins. It's a good idea to get rid of that foamy stuff before cooking them, so be sure to give them a good rinse. You can either rinse them in cold, running water until the water is clear or place them into a bowl with enough water to cover and rub them with your hands to wash off the foam. Then drain them and repeat the process until the water is mostly clear.

For most of the recipes in this book that call for lentils, you will cook your lentils directly in a curry or chili. But it's good to know how to cook lentils separately in case you want to add them to a soup, curry, chili, or some other dish you've already made.

Cooking Your Lentils

The ratio of lentils to water is about 2 cups water (or vegetable broth) for each cup of dried lentils. Depending on the type of lentil, you may need to add more liquid as they cook.

Add the lentils and water to a saucepan large enough for the quantity of lentils you are making. Bring the liquid to a boil. Reduce the heat to a simmer and cook your lentils, covered, until al dente, about 20 minutes, depending on the type of lentil.

Soaking Your Cashews

Cashews are a vegan staple. They can be used to make dressings, sauces, dips, vegan cheese, and a gazillion other weirdo vegan alternatives. But, unless you own a good-quality high-speed blender, they need to be soaked before you blend those suckers. That's if you want them to be creamy, which, trust me, you always do. There's nothing worse than a gritty cheese sauce. Okay, sure there is. But still, it's not that hard to soak nuts! (If you own one of those fancy high-speed blenders, and I highly recommend investing in one, it's not necessary to presoak. Though I will admit, I still sometimes do. Some habits are hard to break.)

The Quick Hot-Water Soak (My Go-To Method)

- Bring a pot of water to a roaring boil. Turn off the heat and toss in the cashews. Cover the pot and leave the cashews to soak for at least 30 minutes. Drain and rinse your cashews. They're ready to blend!

The Overnight Soak

- Add the cashews to a bowl with enough water to cover. Allow them to soak overnight or for at least 8 hours. Drain and rinse your cashews. They're ready to blend!

The Desperate Soak

- Add the cashews to a pot with enough water to cover by at least 2 inches. Bring the water to a boil. Boil your cashews for 15 minutes, adding more water as needed. Drain and rinse your cashews. They're ready to blend!

Toasting Your Sesame Seeds

You don't have to toast your sesame seeds before using them in a recipe, and if you're rushing to get dinner on the table, skip this step and use them raw. But if you have a bit of time, do it! Toasting these itty-bitty seeds hugely enhances their flavor and crunchy texture.

Skillet Method

Place the sesame seeds in a dry skillet over medium heat and toast for about 3 minutes, or until they are golden and fragrant. Stir constantly as they easily burn.

How to Safely Puree Hot Sauces & Chilis in a Blender

Several of the recipes in this cookbook call for the partial blending of hot sauces or chilis to obtain a smoother or creamier texture for the final dish. This process can be hazardous if caution is not taken. These steps should be followed:

- Remove the center cap from the lid of the blender.

- Fill the blender no more than halfway.

- Place a towel over the top of the blender to cover the hole. Hold the towel in place with your hand around the edges of the hole.

- Blend the sauce or chili.

- Pour the pureed sauce or chili into the saucepan or a bowl.

- Repeat with the remaining sauce or chili.

- Return the pureed sauce or chili to the saucepan, or as directed in the recipe.

Recipe Jargon

Drain & Rinse

I'm talking about your canned beans and the like. Simply pour the contents into a strainer and rinse them under running water. This removes the excess liquid and gives them a good cleaning. Don't do this for every recipe with beans. Just the ones where I tell you to. Like Simon Says!

Fork-Tender

Usually mentioned in reference to vegetables, especially potatoes, this means you can poke them with the tines of a fork without them screaming at you. The fork meets no resistance and slides easily. That's how we know they're ready.

Neutral-Flavored Oil

These oils won't affect the final taste of the dish and botch it up. When you see this in a recipe, go grab your avocado, canola, corn, grapeseed, refined olive, safflower, sesame, soybean, sunflower, or vegetable oil.

Salt to Taste

While salt is needed to bring out the flavors in a dish, too much isn't good for us. Salt content varies with different brands of ingredients, such as with soy sauce, veggie broth, canned tomatoes, bread crumbs, and canned beans, and this affects the saltiness of the dish. That's why I prefer that you taste what you're making towards the end, and add salt as needed for your particular taste buds.

Chapter 1

Pasta

Saucy, creamy, meaty, garlicky, buttery—pasta comes in all shapes, flavors, textures, and sizes, and this chapter captures them all.

Pasta, one of the ultimate comfort foods, is frequently villainized as being nutritionally empty or blamed for weight gain. While white pasta is classified as a refined grain, meaning it has been stripped of some of its healthy components— fiber being the main one—it is still enriched with B vitamins and iron and contains a reasonable amount of protein. Certainly, whole-wheat pasta is a far healthier option that is rich in fiber, vitamins, minerals, and protein, but indulging in some white pasta now and then shouldn't be shunned, especially when it's served with a healthful sauce and bulked up with veggies.

Lentil Bolognese

1 tablespoon olive oil, plus more
  as needed

1 large yellow onion, diced small

2 medium carrots, diced large

1 celery stalk, sliced crosswise,
  about ¼-inch-thick

2 (8-ounce) packages baby
  bella (cremini) or white button
  mushrooms, sliced

2½ cups vegetable broth, plus
  more as needed

3 garlic cloves, minced

½ teaspoon dried basil

½ teaspoon dried oregano

½ teaspoon dried rosemary

½ teaspoon dried thyme

¼ cup tomato paste

1 (28-ounce) can diced tomatoes

1 cup dried brown lentils

½ teaspoon baking soda

16 ounces spaghetti

Maple syrup to taste

Balsamic vinegar to taste

Salt and freshly ground black
  pepper to taste

The umami quality of mushrooms makes them a fitting ingredient for this Bolognese sauce. Complemented by the thick, almost chewy texture of the brown lentils, this sauce is "meaty" and delicious.

Lentils are loaded with protein and fiber. Plus they cook pretty quickly and don't require soaking. Sometimes, I add a little baking soda to the sauce to tone down the acidity of the tomatoes. Sugar does the same thing but it will also sweeten the sauce.

This is practically a one-pot meal. (Okay. There is a second pot for the pasta, but that doesn't really count. I'll even wash that one for you if you like.)

Serves 4

Heat the olive oil in a large skillet over medium-high heat. Add the onion and cook for about 5 minutes, or until translucent. Add the carrots, celery, and mushrooms and sauté for 7 to 10 minutes, until the mushrooms have released their moisture and browned, adding more olive oil as needed to prevent sticking.

Add ½ cup of the vegetable broth and deglaze the skillet, scraping any browned bits from the sides and bottom of the skillet into the vegetables.

Add the garlic, basil, oregano, rosemary, and thyme and cook for another 30 seconds. Add the tomato paste and cook for 1 minute more, stirring constantly. Mix in the diced tomatoes, lentils, baking soda, and the remaining 2 cups vegetable broth. Bring to a boil, then reduce the heat. Cover and simmer for about 30 minutes, or until the sauce thickens and the lentils are tender. Stir occasionally, adding more vegetable broth if needed to keep the lentils covered.

Meanwhile, cook the spaghetti according to the package directions until it is al dente. Drain and set aside.

Once the lentils are cooked, stir in maple syrup and balsamic vinegar to taste and season with salt and pepper. Mix in the desired amount of cooked spaghetti and continue cooking just until warmed through.

Tofu Bolognese

1 (14-ounce) block **extra-firm tofu**, pressed and crumbled (see page 34)

1½ tablespoons **low-sodium tamari or soy sauce**

3 tablespoons **nutritional yeast**

1½ teaspoons **chili powder**

1½ teaspoons **smoked paprika**

1½ teaspoons **chipotle powder**

¾ teaspoon **garlic powder**

1½ tablespoons **olive oil**

16 ounces **spaghetti**

1 (24-ounce) jar **marinara sauce**

Salt and freshly ground black pepper to taste

1 cup **fresh basil leaves**, chiffonade (thinly sliced), for garnish

You won't miss the meat while chowing down on this Bolognese. In fact, you'll think it's in there. This foolproof method transforms tofu into an ideal ground meat substitute by pressing, crumbling, browning, and seasoning the heck out of it.

My kids love this recipe so much that they've committed it to memory. They make it for friends and family all the time. Not to belittle their culinary expertise, but it's that easy of a recipe. No chopping required.

It's also a very nutritious one. You get a decent amount of plant-based protein and healthy fats from the tofu, B vitamins from the nutritional yeast, and lots of lycopene from the marinara sauce. Lycopene is what gives tomatoes that brilliant red-lipstick color. It's a very powerful antioxidant, and research shows that it may help lower the risk of several cancers as well as strokes. It's better absorbed when combined with some fat, so pairing it with tofu is an excellent idea!

Make sure to take the time to press your tofu before crumbling. This will allow for better browning in the oven and a more meat-like texture.

Serves 4 to 5

Preheat the oven to 400°F. Line a large baking sheet with parchment paper or a silicone mat.

Transfer the crumbled tofu to a medium bowl. Set aside.

In a small bowl, combine the tamari, nutritional yeast, chili powder, smoked paprika, chipotle, garlic powder, and olive oil. Spoon this marinade over the tofu and use your hands to rub the marinade on the crumbles until they are evenly coated.

Spread the crumbles in an even layer on the prepared baking sheet and bake for 15 minutes. Remove the sheet from the oven and toss the crumbles so they cook evenly on all sides. Return the sheet to the oven and cook for about another 10 minutes, or until the crumbles are browned. Change the oven setting to broil and cook for about 2 minutes more, or until the crumbles are crispy. (Keep checking on them so they do not burn.)

Recipe continues

Meanwhile, cook the spaghetti according to the package directions until it is al dente. Drain and set aside. Pour the marinara sauce into a large saucepan set over medium heat. Bring the sauce to a simmer. Add the baked tofu crumbles to the sauce and stir to combine, then simmer for 5 minutes. Mix in the desired amount of cooked spaghetti and continue cooking until warmed through. Season with salt and pepper. Garnish with basil.

Sneaky Veggie Pasta

16 ounces **dry pasta** (rigatoni, penne, spaghetti)

1 tablespoon plus 2 teaspoons **olive oil**

1 medium **yellow onion**, diced

2 medium **zucchini**, peeled, cut into ½-inch-thick rounds, and quartered (about 2⅓ cups)

5 **garlic cloves**, minced

¼ teaspoon **onion powder**

¼ teaspoon **garlic powder**

¼ teaspoon **paprika**

1 tablespoon **mellow (white) miso**

¼ cup **unsweetened nondairy milk**

2½ teaspoons **apple cider vinegar**

3 tablespoons **nutritional yeast**

¼ teaspoon **finely ground black pepper**

⅛ teaspoon **kala namak** (optional)

Salt

Crushed red pepper, for serving (optional)

This pasta gets its name from the fact that it's hard to know which veggie is in the sauce. Or that any veggie is in the sauce. My kids had no idea that they were eating their almost least favorite veggie (zucchini) as they polished off this dish.

Blending the zucchini into the sauce gives it a creamy texture, but because it's nut-free, it doesn't end up quite as creamy as cashew-based sauces. If you want that extra creaminess, soak ¼ cup raw cashews (see page 39) beforehand and add the drained and rinsed cashews to the blender with the zucchini and onion.

A pinch of kala namak is added to re-create the eggy aroma of a Carbonara. Although this ingredient is optional, I highly recommend keeping some in your pantry for adding an egg-like quality to vegan dishes (see page 23).

Remember to save that pasta cooking water.

Serves 4

Cook the pasta according to the package directions until it is al dente. Reserve ½ cup of the pasta cooking water, then drain the pasta. Set aside.

Heat 1 tablespoon of the olive oil in a large skillet over medium heat. Add the onion and zucchini and cook for about 10 minutes, or until the zucchini starts to soften. Add the garlic and cook for another 30 seconds. Add the onion powder, garlic powder, and paprika and cook for 1 minute more.

In a small bowl, stir the miso into 1 tablespoon warm water until completely dissolved. Set aside.

Transfer the cooked onion and zucchini to a blender. Add the nondairy milk, cider vinesgar, nutritional yeast, dissolved miso, black pepper, kala namak (if using), ½ teaspoon salt, and the remaining 2 teaspoons olive oil. Blend until smooth.

Return the blended sauce to a large saucepan and add ¼ cup of the reserved pasta cooking water. Add the desired amount of cooked pasta. Cook over medium heat for about 5 minutes, or until warmed through, stirring frequently. Add more of the reserved pasta water as needed until the desired consistency. Add salt to taste. Sprinkle crushed red pepper, if using, on top before serving.

Creamy One-Pot Cheesy Broccoli Pasta Soup

Soup and pasta in one. What could be cozier? And this time there really is just one pot to clean. No one wants to eat a big bowl of pasta, the ultimate comfort food, and then wash multiple pots. That would be so uncomforting.

The cheesy flavor in this dish comes from the nutritional yeast, which also packs in those essential B vitamins.

Serves 2

1 tablespoon **olive oil**

1 small **yellow onion**, diced small

2 **garlic cloves**, minced

½ teaspoon **ground mustard seed**

2 cups bite-size **broccoli florets**

2 tablespoons **all-purpose flour**

3 cups **vegetable broth**, plus up to 1 cup more as needed

1 tablespoon **low-sodium tamari or soy sauce**

3 tablespoons **nutritional yeast**

2 cups **dry pasta** (farfalle, orecchiette, radiatori, or rotini)

Salt and freshly ground black pepper to taste

Heat the olive oil in a large nonstick sauté pan over medium heat. Add the onion and cook for about 5 minutes, or until translucent. Add the garlic and ground mustard and cook for 30 seconds more, stirring constantly. Add the broccoli, stirring the florets, onion, and garlic together, and cook for another 30 seconds.

Add the flour and mix well to coat the broccoli. Cook for 1 to 2 minutes, until the broccoli is evenly coated with the flour, stirring constantly.

Add the vegetable broth, tamari, and nutritional yeast. Stir until all the ingredients are fully incorporated, mixing well so that the flour does not become lumpy.

Add the pasta and bring the cooking liquid to a boil. Reduce the heat to low, cover, and simmer for about 10 minutes, or until the pasta is al dente. Stir frequently to avoid the pasta from sticking. Add more broth as needed to cover the pasta.

When the pasta is al dente, season with salt and pepper.

One-Pot Nut-Free Creamy Spaghetti

Here's another one-pot pasta, because whoever's on dishes loves them!

The creamy texture of this sauce comes from the grape tomatoes bursting and combining with the nondairy milk—no cashews or coconut milk needed. Don't get me wrong, I love coconut milk and cashews, but I feel they are used a bit too often in vegan recipes, so I like to suggest alternatives.

I love topping this pasta with Chickpea Croutons (page 222) for more protein and fiber.

Serves 4 to 5

1 tablespoon olive oil

1 large or 2 medium shallots, diced small (about ½ cup)

3 garlic cloves, minced

½ teaspoon crushed red pepper, or to taste

2 tablespoons tomato paste

1 pint grape tomatoes, halved

Salt and freshly ground black pepper to taste

2½ cups unsweetened nondairy milk

2½ cups vegetable broth, plus more as needed

16 ounces spaghetti

⅓ cup nutritional yeast or vegan Parmesan cheese

1 cup fresh basil leaves, thinly sliced

Heat the olive oil in a large nonstick sauté pan over medium heat. Add the shallots and cook for about 3 minutes, or until softened and golden brown. Add the garlic and crushed red pepper and cook for another 30 seconds. Mix in the tomato paste and cook for 30 seconds more, stirring constantly.

Add the grape tomatoes and cook for about 6 minutes, or until they start to release their juices. Season the tomatoes with a generous pinch of salt and pepper.

Add the nondairy milk, vegetable broth, and spaghetti and stir until the pasta is submerged in the liquid. Bring the liquid to a boil, then reduce the heat. Cover and simmer for about 10 minutes, or until the pasta is al dente. Stir every 2 to 3 minutes to make sure the spaghetti does not stick. Add more vegetable broth, as needed, once the pasta is al dente until the desired texture.

Stir in the nutritional yeast and fresh basil. Use a pair of tongs to incorporate the ingredients evenly. (They're also handy for dishing out the food.)

Season with salt and pepper.

Sun-Dried Tomato Hummus Pasta

8 ounces **dry pasta** (farfalle, rigatoni, paccheri)

2 teaspoons **olive oil**

1 small **yellow onion**, thinly sliced (about 1½ cups)

6 **sun-dried tomato halves**, chopped

3 **garlic cloves**, minced

½ teaspoon **crushed red pepper** (optional)

½ teaspoon **paprika**

1 cup **hummus**, store-bought or homemade (see page 251)

Salt and freshly ground black pepper to taste

2 to 3 tablespoons chopped **fresh parsley**, for garnish

This pasta comes together superfast if you use store-bought hummus. Most types of store-bought hummus will work, but if you choose to make your own, I suggest Light & Fluffy Hummus (page 251).

The creamy hummus gives this sauce its smooth and delicious texture, plus it adds healthy fats and protein to the dish. The sun-dried tomatoes add a unique and delicious sweet-tart flavor. They're also rich in vitamins, minerals, and antioxidants, particularly lycopene, which is a powerful antioxidant. Antioxidants stabilize free radicals that come from the environment. Free radicals damage cells and, in high levels, have been linked to several health conditions. That is why lycopene is thought to reduce the risk of developing several chronic illnesses, including cancer.

Try to find the sun-dried tomato halves that come in a jar, packed in olive oil. If you can't find these in your supermarket, any jar or canned version will do.

Remember to save your pasta cooking water. It adds to the creamy texture of the sauce.

Serves 2 to 3

Cook the pasta according to the package directions until it is al dente. Reserve 1 cup of the pasta cooking water, then drain the pasta. Set aside.

Heat the olive oil in a large skillet over medium heat. Add the onion and cook for about 5 minutes, or until golden brown. Add the sun-dried tomatoes and cook for 3 minutes more. Add the garlic, crushed red pepper (if using), and paprika and cook for 1 more minute, stirring constantly.

Add ½ cup of the pasta cooking water and the hummus to the skillet. Mix to incorporate. Cook for about 1 minute, or until the sauce is heated through. Mix in the cooked pasta and cook for about 1 minute more, or until heated through, adding more of the reserved pasta cooking water as needed for the desired consistency.

Season with salt and pepper. Garnish with parsley.

Mushroom Tahini Pasta

1½ cups **dry pasta** (farfalle, fusilli, penne, radiatori)

2 tablespoons **tahini**

2 teaspoons **low-sodium tamari or soy sauce**

2 teaspoons **olive oil**

½ **yellow onion**, diced

1 (8-ounce) package **baby bella (cremini) or white button mushrooms**, sliced

2 **garlic cloves**, minced

¼ teaspoon **five-spice seasoning**

¼ teaspoon **crushed red pepper**

½ cup **vegetable broth**, plus more as needed

Salt and freshly ground black pepper to taste

3 tablespoons chopped **fresh parsley**, for garnish

Tahini is one of my most cherished ingredients. It makes sauces creamy; it has good fats from the sesame seeds; it adds a distinct and delicious flavor; and it's readily available. It's so good with pasta, lentils, and beans. What's not to love?

Five-spice powder lends a distinct flavor that complements the tahini perfectly. It's a blend of cinnamon, fennel, cloves, star anise, and white pepper. While it's not a pantry staple for this cookbook, I highly recommend having some on hand. It's quite versatile and a common ingredient in Chinese cooking. I like that it encompasses all five tastes: sweet, sour, bitter, salty, and umami. Having said that, if you don't have any, you can absolutely make this recipe without it. Don't forget to save that pasta water; it makes a great sauce thickener.

Serves 2 to 3

Cook the pasta according to the package directions until it is al dente. Reserve ¼ cup of the pasta cooking water, then drain the pasta. Set aside.

In a small bowl, mix the reserved pasta cooking water, tahini, and tamari until smooth. Set aside.

Heat the olive oil in a medium nonstick skillet over medium heat. Add the onion and mushrooms and cook for about 5 minutes, or until the mushrooms release their water. Add the garlic, five-spice seasoning, and crushed red pepper and cook for about 30 seconds more, or until fragrant, stirring constantly.

Add the vegetable broth and cook for 2 more minutes, or until the broth is warm.

Reduce the heat to low and stir in the tahini mixture. Cook for about 2 minutes more, or until the sauce thickens, adding more vegetable broth as needed for the desired consistency. Turn off the heat. Mix in the cooked pasta.

Season with salt and pepper. Garnish with parsley.

Tomato Zucchini Pasta

16 ounces **dry pasta** (spaghetti, penne, rigatoni)

½ (14-ounce) block **silken tofu**

2 tablespoons **olive oil**

2 large **zucchini**, cut into half moons, about ¾-inch-thick

8 **garlic cloves**, minced

2 tablespoons **tomato paste**

1 (28-ounce) can **diced tomatoes**

1 teaspoon **maple syrup**

2 teaspoons **Dijon mustard**

1 tablespoon plus 1 teaspoon **low-sodium tamari or soy sauce**

1 tablespoon **freshly squeezed lemon juice**

Salt and freshly ground black pepper to taste

I'm all about substitutions. Being able to use what I already have on hand is how I like to roll. So don't skip over this recipe because you don't have any zucchini, or because you simply can't stand them. Most veggies will be happy to take their place. Use about 2 cups bite-size pieces of your choice veggie in place of the zucchini.

My favorite substitution is white or cremini mushrooms. Okay, they're technically fungi. To substitute for mushrooms, use 2 (8-ounce) packages baby bella (cremini) or white button mushrooms, quartered.

This recipe uses silken tofu for a rich, creamy nut-free sauce.

Serves 5

Cook the pasta according to the package directions until it is al dente. Drain and set aside.

Transfer the tofu to a blender and blend until smooth. Set aside.

Heat the olive oil in a large nonstick skillet over medium-high heat. Add the zucchini and sauté for about 4 minutes, or until it starts to brown. Add the garlic and cook for 30 seconds more. Add the tomato paste and cook for another 30 seconds, stirring constantly.

Add the diced tomatoes, maple syrup, mustard, and tamari and stir to combine. Mix in the blended tofu gradually, stirring until the sauce is sufficiently creamy, and simmer gently for 2 to 3 minutes, until warmed through. Add the lemon juice. Stir in the desired amount of cooked pasta.

Season with salt and pepper.

Fire-Roasted Rigatoni alla Vodka

16 ounces **rigatoni**

1 tablespoon **olive oil**

1 large **yellow onion**, diced (about 2¼ cups)

5 **garlic cloves**, minced

1 teaspoon **dried basil**

1 teaspoon **dried oregano**

½ teaspoon **dried thyme**

½ teaspoon **crushed red pepper**

1 tablespoon **tomato paste**

1 (28-ounce) can **fire-roasted tomatoes**

1 (28-ounce) can **diced tomatoes**

1 cup **vodka**

1 cup **raw cashews**, soaked, drained, and rinsed (see page 39)

Salt and freshly ground black pepper to taste

1 cup **fresh basil leaves**, thinly sliced (chiffonade), for garnish

Traditionally, this dish is known as penne alla vodka, but I don't see why a sauce this delicious should be limited to penne. I often make mine with rigatoni, although my favorite pasta shape is radiatori. It has a large surface area to soak up the sauce, and a unique shape. Try and get your hands on some and make yourself radiatori alla vodka!

The vodka in the sauce releases flavors from the tomatoes that are normally inaccessible, adding even more depth to the dish. We are doubling down on flavor here by also adding fire-roasted tomatoes. These tomatoes are charred over a flame before they are diced, bringing out the tomatoes' sweetness and imparting a distinct smokiness.

A note to grown-ups: While the consensus seems to be that it's safe to serve vodka sauce to kids, I suggest keeping this recipe for adults only. There's quite a bit of vodka in this sauce!

Serves 5

Cook the pasta according to the package directions until it is al dente. Drain and set aside.

Meanwhile, heat the olive oil in a large saucepan over medium heat. Add the onion and cook for about 7 minutes, or until translucent. Add the garlic, dried basil, oregano, thyme, and crushed red pepper. Cook for 1 minute more. Add the tomato paste and mix to combine. Cook for 1 minute, stirring constantly.

Add the fire-roasted tomatoes, diced tomatoes, and vodka and stir. Bring the sauce to a gentle boil, then reduce the heat to a simmer. Cook for 15 minutes.

Allow the sauce to cool before transferring it to a high-speed blender. Add the cashews. Blend on high until smooth. (You may have to blend the sauce in batches depending on the size of your blender.)

Return the sauce to the saucepan and stir in the cooked pasta. Heat for about 4 minutes, or until warmed through. Season with salt and pepper. Garnish with basil.

Creamy Corn Pasta

16 ounces **dry pasta** (spaghetti, penne, rigatoni)

½ cup **raw cashews**, soaked, drained, and rinsed (see page 39)

Salt

4 tablespoons **vegan butter**

4 cups **frozen corn kernels**

2 **garlic cloves**, minced

2 tablespoons **fresh thyme leaves**, or 2 teaspoons **dried thyme**

1 teaspoon **garlic powder**

¾ teaspoon **crushed red pepper**, or to taste

½ teaspoon **smoked paprika**

Freshly ground black pepper to taste

¼ cup chopped **fresh parsley**, for garnish

The creaminess of this pasta is accentuated by the starch from both the corn and the pasta cooking water. Take note, friends: Pasta cooking water is an easy and effective way to add texture to a sauce. You just need to remember to save some. I forget all the time and then I have to make more pasta just for the water. My kids love when this happens, as they get double servings of pasta!

The sweet corn and cashews give this sauce just the right amount of sweetness, balanced by the smoky paprika flavor. This is high on the list of recipes my kids ask me to make over and over again. Did I mention that I'm addicted to this subtly sweet, guilt-free cream?

Serves 5

Cook the pasta according to the package directions until it is al dente. Reserve 2 cups of the pasta cooking water, then drain the pasta. Set aside.

Place the cashews in a high-speed blender. Add ¼ cup water and ¼ teaspoon salt. Blend on high until smooth, adding more water as needed for a smoother consistency.

Place the butter in a large skillet over medium-high heat. Once the butter melts, add the corn and cook 5 to 8 minutes, until the corn has browned.

Stir in the garlic, thyme, garlic powder, crushed red pepper, and smoked paprika. Add a generous dash of salt. Cook for 1 minute.

Stir in the cashew cream and reserved pasta cooking water. Cook on medium-high heat for 3 to 4 minutes, until the sauce has thickened. Stir in the desired amount of cooked pasta and cook for 2 to 3 minutes more, until the pasta is heated through. Use a pair of tongs while heating the pasta to incorporate it with the corn and sauce. Season with salt and pepper. Garnish with parsley.

Eggplant Parmesan Meatballs

Eggplant gets a new look with these delicious crispy meatballs. Eggplant has a decent amount of potassium and fiber. It is also rich in plant-based micronutrients called polyphenols, which are believed to help the body do a better job of processing sugar. This is especially beneficial if you have diabetes.

These meatballs have a delicious, cheesy flavor from the nutritional yeast, which means they're also rich in essential B vitamins. If you follow a strictly vegan diet, it's vital to get those Bs, even if it means taking a B_{12} supplement.

Serves 3 (makes 15 meatballs)

3 tablespoons olive oil

1 medium eggplant (about 12 ounces), peeled and cut into ½-inch cubes

1 medium yellow onion, minced

6 garlic cloves, minced

1 tablespoon dried basil

1 teaspoon dried oregano

½ teaspoon dried thyme

¼ teaspoon finely ground black pepper

2 tablespoons nutritional yeast

1 cup dried bread crumbs

¾ teaspoon salt, or to taste

16 ounces spaghetti

1 (24-ounce) jar marinara sauce

¼ cup chopped fresh parsley, for garnish

Preheat the oven to 400°F. Line a baking sheet with parchment paper or a silicone mat. Set aside.

Heat the olive oil in a large skillet over medium heat. Add the eggplant and cook, occasionally mashing it with the side of a spatula or wooden spoon, for about 5 minutes, or until the eggplant starts to become tender. Add the onion and cook for 4 to 5 minutes more, until the eggplant is cooked through and tender but still holds its shape.

Add the garlic, basil, oregano, thyme, and black pepper and cook for 30 seconds.

Transfer the eggplant mixture to a large bowl. Mix in the nutritional yeast and bread crumbs. (Bread crumbs contain different amounts of sodium, so it is important to taste the eggplant mixture before adding the salt.) Taste the mixture and season with the salt. Allow the mixture to sit at room temperature until cool enough to handle before forming the meatballs.

Using your hands and about 1½ tablespoons of the eggplant mixture for each, form 15 meatballs. Place the meatballs on the prepared baking sheet and bake for 15 minutes. Flip them over and cook for about 10 minutes more, or until golden brown on both sides.

Meanwhile, cook the spaghetti according to the package directions until it is al dente and heat the marinara sauce in a medium saucepan over medium heat.

Allow the meatballs to cool for about 10 minutes. Transfer them to the saucepan with the marinara sauce. Heat gently until warmed through before serving on top of the pasta and garnishing with parsley.

Chickpeas & Broccoli in Béchamel Sauce

16 ounces **dry pasta** (farfalle, orecchiette, spaghetti, fusilli)

Béchamel Sauce

1 cup **raw cashews**, soaked, drained, and rinsed (see page 39)

⅓ cup **nutritional yeast**

1 tablespoon **garlic powder**

1 teaspoon **salt**, or to taste

½ teaspoon **onion powder**

⅛ teaspoon **ground nutmeg**

⅛ teaspoon **finely ground black pepper**

1 large head **broccoli**, cut into bite-size florets (about 3 cups)

2 cups **cooked chickpeas**, or about 1½ (15-ounce) cans chickpeas, drained and rinsed

1 tablespoon plus 1 teaspoon **olive oil** (optional)

Salt

Freshly ground black pepper to taste

Vegan cheese shreds (optional)

Béchamel is essentially a creamy white sauce. It's typically dairy-based and thickened with flour and butter. This vegan version uses cashews for the creamy base and nutritional yeast for a "cheesy" flavor, with an added benefit of fortifying the sauce with those essential B vitamins.

There is an optional step for making the chickpeas crispy before adding them to the sauce. If you are short on time, you can skip this step and add the chickpeas without sautéing them.

Serves 4

Cook the pasta according to the package directions until it is al dente. Drain and set aside.

Make the béchamel sauce: Blend the cashews, nutritional yeast, garlic powder, salt, onion powder, nutmeg, black pepper, and 1½ cups water in a high-speed blender on high until smooth. Set aside.

Place the broccoli florets in a steamer basket. Add about 1 inch of water to a large saucepan and bring it to a boil over medium heat. Once the water is boiling, reduce the heat to a gentle boil and place the steamer basket and broccoli inside. Cover with a tight-fitting lid and steam for about 5 minutes, or until the florets are fork-tender. (Alternatively, if you have a microwave, you can place the broccoli in a microwave-safe bowl with 3 tablespoons water, cover the bowl, and microwave for 2 to 3 minutes, or until just tender.) Transfer the broccoli to a colander. Set aside.

To make crispy chickpeas, if desired, place the chickpeas in a medium bowl. Add the olive oil and ¼ teaspoon salt. Using your hands, rub the chickpeas until they are evenly coated with the oil. Transfer the chickpeas to a large nonstick skillet over medium-high heat and sauté for about 5 minutes, or until golden brown. Transfer the chickpeas to a large plate. (Alternatively, use drained and rinsed chickpeas in the next step.)

Heat the sauce in a large saucepan over medium-low heat, stirring constantly. Once the sauce starts to thicken, add the chickpeas and broccoli and cook until heated through. Season with salt and pepper.

Stir in the desired amount of cooked pasta and serve with vegan cheese shreds, if using.

Miso Sweet Potato Pasta with Sage

8 ounces **dry pasta** (penne, rigatoni, paccheri)

1 medium **sweet potato**

2 teaspoons plus 1 tablespoon **olive oil**

5 **fresh sage leaves**

2 tablespoons **chopped pecans**

2 tablespoons **raw pepitas** (shelled pumpkin seeds)

3 large **garlic cloves**, minced

2 teaspoons **mellow (white) miso**

½ cup **unsweetened nondairy milk**

½ cup **vegetable broth**

1 teaspoon **low-sodium tamari or soy sauce**

1 tablespoon **freshly squeezed lime juice**

Salt and freshly ground black pepper to taste

Baked sweet potatoes have a velvety texture that, when blended, will transform your pasta sauce into one that is extra creamy and delicious.

The salty and umami flavors of the miso combined with the tanginess of the lime juice perfectly balance the sweetness of the sweet potato. Miso needs to be dissolved in water before adding it to the sauce. You really don't want lumps of miso in your pasta. For a nut-free recipe, omit the pecans.

Serves 3

Preheat the oven to 425°F. Line a small baking sheet with parchment paper, if desired, for easier cleanup.

Cook the pasta according to the package directions until it is al dente. Drain and set aside.

Pierce the sweet potato all over with a fork and transfer it to the prepared baking sheet. Bake for about 45 minutes, or until easily pierced with a fork in the thickest part. Allow the sweet potato to cool before slicing it in half lengthwise.

While the sweet potato is baking, heat 2 teaspoons of the olive oil in a small skillet over medium-high heat. Add the sage leaves and cook for about 3 minutes, or until they are crispy. Transfer the leaves to a plate.

Add the remaining 1 tablespoon olive oil to the same skillet. Heat the oil over medium heat. Add the pecans and pepitas and cook them for about 3 minutes, or until they start to brown, stirring constantly. Add the garlic and cook for about 1 minute more, or until the garlic is fragrant. Set aside.

In a small bowl, stir the miso into 1 tablespoon warm water until completely dissolved. Set aside.

Scoop out 1 cup of the cooled sweet potato flesh and transfer it to a blender. Add the fried sage leaves, nondairy milk, vegetable broth, and dissolved miso. Blend the sweet potato mixture on high until smooth. Transfer the blended sauce to a medium saucepan.

Heat the sauce over medium-low heat until warmed through. Stir in the tamari and lime juice. Add the cooked pasta and mix until the pasta is completely coated with the sauce. Mix in the sautéed pecans, pepitas, and garlic. Season with salt and pepper.

Mushroom Stroganoff

8 ounces **dry pasta** (rigatoni, paccheri, penne)

1 tablespoon **olive oil**

1 medium **shallot**, chopped (about ½ cup)

3 large **garlic cloves**, minced

1 (8-ounce) package **baby bella (cremini) mushrooms**, stems trimmed, chopped

2 teaspoons chopped **fresh sage leaves, or** ½ teaspoon **ground sage**

½ cup dry **white wine or vegetable broth**

2¾ cups **vegetable broth**

½ cup **raw cashews**, soaked, drained, and rinsed (see page 39)

2 tablespoons **low-sodium tamari or soy sauce**

½ teaspoon **balsamic vinegar**

Salt and freshly ground black pepper to taste

1½ tablespoons chopped **fresh parsley**, for garnish

Stroganoff is traditionally made with beef, and butter, flour, and sour cream are added for a creamy sauce. We are using blended cashews to achieve that same creaminess and capitalizing on the umami quality and the silky, meat-like texture of mushrooms to give us that same meaty feel.

While beef stroganoff is usually served with egg noodles, I enjoy mine with either pasta or a side of potatoes. To change things up, skip the pasta and enjoy your stroganoff with Smashed Potatoes (page 227) or Crispy Top Potato Rounds (page 229).

Make sure to use a good quality dry white wine for this recipe, one that you enjoy drinking. Otherwise, substitute the wine for vegetable broth.

Did I mention how creamy and flavorful this dish is? Oh . . . and the smell is tantalizing.

Serves 2 to 3

Cook the pasta according to the package directions until it is al dente. Drain and set aside.

Heat the olive oil in a large saucepan or Dutch oven over medium heat. Add the shallot and cook for 1 minute. Add the garlic and cook for another 30 seconds. Add the mushrooms and sage and cook for 6 to 8 minutes, until the mushrooms soften and release their water, stirring occasionally.

Add the wine and deglaze the saucepan using a wooden spoon, scraping the browned bits from the sides and bottom of the pan. Add 2 cups of the vegetable broth and bring the mixture to a boil, then reduce the heat. Simmer for 10 minutes.

Place the cashews into a high-speed blender with the remaining ¾ cup vegetable broth. Blend on high until smooth.

Transfer the blended cashews to the saucepan with the mushrooms. Add the tamari and balsamic vinegar, stirring to combine. Simmer for about 5 minutes, or until the sauce thickens to the desired consistency. Season with salt and pepper. Mix in the cooked pasta. Garnish with parsley.

Pasta Alfredo with Toasted Pumpkin Seeds

Biting into creamy pasta tossed with toasted pumpkin seeds is one of those "OMG" moments. The crunchy texture of the pumpkin seeds adds a whole other dimension to this dish. They're optional, but I highly recommend adding them. They're also high in fiber and a good source of plant-based protein and healthy fats. And they're packed with magnesium, which is often lacking in Western diets. Magnesium plays many crucial roles in the body, including supporting muscle and nerve function, as well as helping our body to produce energy.

And these pumpkin seeds are not good just in this Alfredo. I love adding them as a garnish to salads, guacamole, and roasted veggies, or sometimes I roast them with a little maple syrup and pumpkin pie spice and eat them as a snack. You won't be sorry about your pumpkin seed investment.

One more thing, friends: this Alfredo sauce is another one of those versatile pasta sauces. It also pairs well with roasted veggies, chickpeas, and potatoes. The umami flavor from the miso, combined with a hint of spice from the sriracha, and the tang from the mustard seeds, give this white sauce a rich and unique taste.

Serves 4

16 ounces **dry pasta** (linguine, fettuccini, spaghetti, rigatoni)

2 tablespoons **olive oil**

½ cup **raw pepitas** (shelled pumpkin seeds), optional

Salt to taste

Alfredo Sauce

2 tablespoons **mellow (white) miso**

¾ cup **raw cashews**, soaked, drained, and rinsed (see page 39)

¼ cup **cornstarch**

2 **garlic cloves**, chopped

2 teaspoons **freshly squeezed lemon juice**

½ teaspoon **sriracha**

½ teaspoon **ground mustard seed**

Freshly ground black pepper to taste

Cook the pasta according to the package directions until it is al dente. Drain and set aside.

If using the pepitas, heat the olive oil in a medium skillet over medium-high heat. Add the pepitas and cook for about 3 minutes, or until puffed and browned, stirring constantly. Transfer the toasted pepitas to a paper-towel-lined plate. Season with salt and set aside.

Make the Alfredo sauce: In a small bowl, stir the miso into 2 tablespoons warm water until completely dissolved. Combine the cashews, cornstarch, dissolved miso, garlic, lemon juice, sriracha, ground mustard, and 1½ cups warm water in a high-speed blender. Blend on high until smooth.

Pour the Alfredo sauce into a medium saucepan and cook over low heat for about 30 seconds, or until the sauce just starts to thicken, whisking constantly. Stir in the desired amount of cooked pasta and continue cooking for about 2 minutes more, or until the sauce has thickened sufficiently to coat the pasta. Season with salt and pepper. Top with the toasted pepitas, and serve immediately.

Chapter 2

Beans & Chili

Full of Beans!

Beans are an indispensable part of any plant-based diet. They're packed with protein, fiber, and an abundance of vitamins and minerals. They help us stay regular, fill our bellies so we don't overeat, and keep our hearts and bodies healthy.

There are innumerable ways to serve your beans. My go-to is to create a balanced bowl with protein-packed beans, a salad or veggie side (see pages 191–222), and a starchy or potato side (see pages 223–244). And when that feels like too much work, you can always count on a simple side of steamed rice.

Some of my favorite bean pairings include:
- Asian-Inspired Crunchy Salad with Sesame Ginger Dressing (page 196)
- Garlicky Kale (page 201) and sliced avocado
- Garlicky Rice (page 235)
- Coconut Quinoa (page 235)
- Lemony Cauliflower Rice (page 237)
- Cornbread Mug Cake (page 244)
- Cheesy Savory Pancakes (page 239)
- Easy Guacamole (page 252) and Pita Chips (page 243)

Sweet Potato Baked Beans

The natural sweetness of sweet potato, the umami quality of miso, and the flavorful and smoky chili spices all come together harmoniously in this recipe.

Take note, friends, you don't want to add miso directly to sauces. You have to dissolve it in water first, or you'll end up with chunks of miso in your sauce, and whomever you make this dish for won't ever let you cook for them again.

You can substitute most other beans for the pintos. Cannellini or navy beans work very well.

These beans are so delicious served on crispy toast with smashed avocado.

Serves 5

1 tablespoon olive oil

1 large yellow onion, diced

3 garlic cloves, minced

1 large sweet potato, peeled and cut into ¾-inch pieces (about 2½ cups)

1 tablespoon chili powder

1 teaspoon smoked paprika

½ teaspoon ground cumin

½ teaspoon dried oregano

¼ teaspoon finely ground black pepper

1 tablespoon tomato paste

1 (14.5-ounce) can diced tomatoes

1 cup vegetable broth

2 tablespoons mellow (white) miso

3 tablespoons nutritional yeast

1 (15-ounce) can pinto beans, drained and rinsed, or 1½ cups cooked beans

2 tablespoons freshly squeezed lime juice

Salt and freshly ground black pepper to taste

Heat the olive oil in a large saucepan over medium heat. Add the onion, garlic, and sweet potato and cook for 3 to 5 minutes, until the onion becomes translucent.

Add the chili powder, smoked paprika, cumin, oregano, and finely ground black pepper and cook for 30 seconds more. Add the tomato paste and cook for 1 more minute, stirring constantly. Add the diced tomatoes and vegetable broth, stir to combine, and bring to a boil. Reduce the heat, cover, and gently simmer for 20 to 25 minutes, until the sweet potato is fork-tender.

Use an immersion blender or a standard blender to puree the sauce mixture until smooth.

In a small bowl, stir the miso into ½ cup warm water until completely dissolved.

Set the blended sauce over medium heat. Add the dissolved miso and nutritional yeast and stir to combine. Mix in the pinto beans. Cook for about 3 minutes more, or just until the beans are warmed through. Add the lime juice. Season with salt and pepper.

Smashed Pinto Beans with Tahini

2 teaspoons **olive oil**

1 medium **yellow onion**, finely diced

2 **garlic cloves**, minced

½ teaspoon **dried oregano**

½ teaspoon **paprika**

¼ teaspoon **chili powder**

¼ teaspoon **ground cumin**

¼ teaspoon **finely ground black pepper**

Pinch of **chipotle powder**

½ cup **tomato sauce**

1 cup **vegetable broth**

1 teaspoon **Dijon mustard**

1 (15-ounce) can **pinto beans**, undrained, or 1½ cups cooked beans plus ½ cup cooking liquid

1 tablespoon **tahini**

¼ cup **chopped walnuts** (optional)

Freshly squeezed lime juice to taste

Salt and freshly ground black pepper to taste

2 tablespoons chopped **fresh cilantro**, for garnish

Tahini and walnuts are superstars when it comes to healthy fats, especially the essential omega-3s. They also lend texture to this dish. Tahini makes these beans creamy, while the chopped walnuts add a delicious crunch. The walnuts are optional, but if you're not allergic to nuts, I encourage you to leave them in there, as they're arguably the healthiest nut!

I enjoy my smashed pintos on sourdough toast with smashed avocado and a dollop of my Sour Cream (page 249). Or use them as a burrito filling with rice, avocado, shredded lettuce, vegan cheese shreds, and vegan mayo.

Serves 3

Heat the olive oil in a medium saucepan over medium heat. Add the onion and garlic and cook for 3 to 5 minutes, stirring frequently, until the onion is translucent.

Add the oregano, paprika, chili powder, cumin, finely ground black pepper, and the chipotle powder. Cook for 30 seconds, stirring constantly. Add the tomato sauce, vegetable broth, mustard, and pinto beans and their liquid and stir. Bring to a boil, then reduce the heat to a gentle boil and cook, uncovered, for about 15 minutes, or until most of the liquid evaporates.

Transfer the bean mixture to a large bowl. Use a potato masher to mash the beans until almost smooth but with some whole beans remaining. Mix in the tahini and walnuts (if using). Stir in the lime juice, season with salt and pepper, and garnish with cilantro.

Coconut Kidney Beans

This dish comes together super fast and is a real crowd-pleaser. It's a good one to have in your repertoire. I enjoy pairing these with a big steaming bowl of rice. Did you know rice and beans make a complete protein? This powerhouse of a combo contains the nine essential amino acids necessary in the human diet.

You can skip the coconut milk if you're not a fan. These beans are still yummy without it. And feel free to substitute black beans for the kidney beans.

Serves 3

1 tablespoon olive oil

1 medium yellow onion, diced small

2 garlic cloves, minced

1½ teaspoons minced fresh ginger

1¼ teaspoons garam masala

1 (14.5-ounce) can crushed tomatoes

1 (15-ounce) can kidney beans, drained and rinsed, or 1½ cups cooked beans

1 teaspoon low-sodium tamari or soy sauce

1 cup unsweetened canned coconut milk, plus more as needed

Salt to taste

¼ cup chopped fresh cilantro, for garnish

1 lime, sliced into wedges, for serving

Heat the olive oil in a medium saucepan over medium-high heat. Add the onion and cook for about 5 minutes, or until translucent. Add the garlic and ginger and cook for another 30 seconds. Add the garam masala and cook for 1 minute more.

Stir in the crushed tomatoes, beans, tamari, and coconut milk. Reduce the heat to a gentle simmer, cover, and cook for 10 minutes, stirring occasionally. Add more coconut milk or water as needed until the desired consistency. (You can also mash some of the beans with a spatula to thicken the sauce.) Add salt to taste, garnish with cilantro, and serve with lime wedges.

Tahini Black Beans

1 tablespoon **olive oil**

1 large **yellow onion**, diced small

3 **garlic cloves**, minced

1 teaspoon **dried oregano**

½ teaspoon **garlic powder**

½ teaspoon **onion powder**

1 tablespoon **tomato paste**

1 (15-ounce) can **black beans**, undrained, or 1½ cups cooked beans plus ½ cup cooking liquid

½ cup **vegetable broth**

1 tablespoon **tahini**

1 tablespoon **Dijon mustard**

1 tablespoon **red wine vinegar or apple cider vinegar**

Salt and freshly ground black pepper to taste

Tahini is one of the most versatile ingredients in your kitchen. I add it to beans, lentils, soups, sauces, and dressings to make them creamier and more satisfying. It's also delicious drizzled over baked sweet potatoes. Made from toasted ground sesame seeds, it is loaded with heart-healthy fats and has a distinct and delicious sesame flavor. It's a pantry must-have!

I often enjoy my Tahini Black Beans with an oversized bowl of Garlicky Rice (page 235), topped with Cabbage Slaw (page 191) and an oversized dollop of Easy Guacamole (page 252).

Serves 3 to 4

Heat the olive oil in a medium saucepan over medium-high heat. Add the onion and cook for about 5 minutes, or until translucent. Add the garlic and cook for 30 seconds more. Add the oregano, garlic powder, and onion powder and cook for 1 more minute.

Stir in the tomato paste, beans and their liquid, and vegetable broth. Reduce the heat, cover, and gently simmer for 5 minutes.

In a small bowl, mix the tahini, mustard, vinegar, and 1 tablespoon water until a smooth paste forms. Remove the beans from the heat and stir in the paste until it is fully incorporated into the sauce. Season with salt and pepper.

Practically Vegan

Taco Pinto Beans in Creamy Tomato Sauce

I make my own taco seasoning for this recipe, which is why it's so darn flavorful. The depth of flavor from the spices perfectly balances the hint of sweetness from the blended cashews, which is what make the sauce deliciously creamy.

Feel free to swap the pintos with other types of beans; black beans, kidney beans, or even lentils will all work. For a less spicy version, leave out the cayenne.

Fill your taco shells with these flavorful beans and serve them alongside Cabbage Slaw (page 191) and smashed avocado with a squeeze of fresh lime.

Serves 3

1 tablespoon **olive oil**

1 small **yellow onion**, diced

2 **garlic cloves**, minced

Taco Seasoning

2 teaspoons **chili powder**

½ teaspoon **smoked paprika**

½ teaspoon **ground cumin**

½ teaspoon **dried oregano**

⅛ teaspoon **cayenne pepper**

⅛ teaspoon **onion powder** (optional)

⅛ teaspoon **garlic powder** (optional)

¼ teaspoon **salt**

¼ teaspoon **finely ground black pepper**

1 tablespoon **tomato paste**

1 cup canned **diced tomatoes**

½ cup **raw cashews**, soaked, drained, and rinsed (see page 39)

1 (15-ounce) can **pinto beans**, undrained, or 1½ cups cooked beans plus ½ cup cooking liquid

Vegetable broth, as needed

Salt and freshly ground black pepper to taste

¼ cup chopped **fresh cilantro**, for garnish

Heat the olive oil in a medium saucepan over medium heat. Add the onion and cook for about 5 minutes, or until translucent. Add the garlic and cook for 30 seconds more.

Make the taco seasoning: In a small bowl, mix the chili powder, smoked paprika, cumin, oregano, cayenne, onion and garlic powders (if using), salt, and black pepper. Add the taco seasoning to the saucepan and cook for 1 more minute, stirring constantly.

Add the tomato paste and cook for 1 minute, stirring constantly. Add the diced tomatoes and bring to a boil before reducing the heat to a gentle simmer. Cover and cook for 5 minutes.

Transfer the sauce to a high-speed blender along with the cashews. Blend on high until smooth. (See page 40 on how to blend hot liquid.)

Return the sauce to the saucepan and add the beans and their liquid. Cook over low heat until the beans and sauce are warmed through, adding vegetable broth as needed for the desired consistency. Season with salt and pepper. Garnish with cilantro.

BBQ Chickpeas

2 teaspoons **olive oil**

½ medium **red onion**, thinly sliced (about 1¼ cups)

1 (15-ounce) can **chickpeas**, drained and rinsed, or 1½ cups cooked chickpeas

BBQ Sauce (page 265)

Salt to taste

Homemade barbecue sauce elevates these sautéed chickpeas to a whole new level of yumminess. Making your own sauce allows you to control how much sugar and salt is in there. Store-bought sauces tend to be quite high in both.

Sautéing your chickpeas until they are golden brown makes them unbearably hard to resist, but seeing as they're a healthy fiber- and protein-rich plant-based food, there's no need to resist! I often eat them straight out of the pan, which means fewer plates to wash!

These chickpeas make it easy to add protein to a dish when you're in a rush to get dinner on the table. My favorite way to eat them, when they do make it out of the pan, is inside a warm Baked Sweet Potato (page 232), topped with smashed avocado, a drizzle of tahini, and a squeeze of fresh lime. Or I use them as a topping for smashed avocado toast.

Serves 3

Heat the olive oil in a medium nonstick skillet over medium-high heat. Add the onion and sauté for about 3 minutes, or until it starts to brown. Add the chickpeas and cook for 3 to 4 minutes, until lightly browned. Reduce the heat to low and stir the BBQ sauce into the chickpeas and onion. Cook for about 2 more minutes, or until the sauce is warmed through. Season with salt.

Chill-i Time

Cozy up to a comforting bowl of protein-packed chili, piled high with your favorite toppings. These chili recipes are anything but boring. From fire-roasted tempeh to potato bean, to mushroom, you're bound to find a healthful chili to rub you the right way.

My exhaustive list of go-to toppings includes, but is not limited to, vegan sour cream, vegan cheese shreds, crushed tortilla chips, avocado chunks, shredded lettuce, sliced olives, guacamole, chopped tomatoes, and spicy salsa. Go to town and make yourself a chili bar!

Or you might want to make yourself a big bowl of chili cheese fries. Top your Crispy Oven Fries (page 180) with a generous serving of chili, some vegan cheese shreds, a dollop of Sour Cream (page 249), and sliced green onions.

And there are other sides and dips to pair with your chili: Cornbread Mug Cake (page 244), Cheesy Savory Pancakes (page 239), Garlicky Rice (page 235), Coconut Quinoa (page 235), Potato Sides (pages 223–234), Garlicky Kale (page 201), Cabbage Slaw (page 191), Sour Cream (page 249), and/or Easy Guacamole (page 252).

In fact, almost anything can be eaten with chili. I've been known to eat mine with pasta when seeking some extra comfort.

Spicy Black Bean Chili

1 tablespoon **olive oil**

1 medium **yellow onion**, diced

3 **garlic cloves**, minced

1¼ teaspoons **chili powder**

1¼ teaspoons **dried basil**

¾ teaspoon **paprika**

¼ to ½ teaspoon **cayenne pepper**, or to taste (optional)

¼ teaspoon **dried oregano**

¼ teaspoon **finely ground black pepper**

3 tablespoons **tomato paste**

1 (14.5-ounce) can **diced tomatoes**

1 (15-ounce) can **black beans**, undrained, or 1½ cups cooked beans plus ½ cup cooking liquid

1 teaspoon **apple cider vinegar**

1 teaspoon **Dijon mustard**

½ teaspoon **maple syrup**

Salt and freshly ground black pepper to taste

Don't get put off by the word *spicy* in the title. You can still make this recipe even if you're not a fan of spicy food: Simply omit or reduce the cayenne. And if you really don't like spice, you can also reduce the amount of chili powder. If you do enjoy spicy food, leave this recipe as is and you will be in chili ecstasy.

While this may be an embarrassingly easy chili recipe, it's absolutely delicious and requires only one pot. In my book, easy, delicious, and one-pot trump all other culinary attributes.

Black bean chili is a classic, but feel free to switch it up and use a different bean. Pinto and kidney beans also work well in this recipe.

Serves 3

Heat the olive oil in a medium saucepan over medium heat. Add the onion and cook for about 5 minutes, or until it starts to turn golden brown. Add the garlic, chili powder, basil, paprika, cayenne (if using), oregano, finely ground black pepper, and the tomato paste. Cook for 1 minute, stirring constantly.

Add the diced tomatoes, black beans with their liquid, cider vinegar, mustard, and maple syrup. Bring to a gentle boil, then reduce the heat. Cover and simmer for 10 minutes. Season with salt and pepper.

Creamy Lentil & Corn Chili

This protein-rich chili is flavorful and easy to make, and the cleanup is a breeze. The sweetness of the corn pairs well with the spice from the jalapeño. (Add the seeds from the jalapeño for an even spicier chili.) I'm definitely a spicy person—both in personality and in flavor preference. My kids are spicy, too, especially my youngest daughter, Asha!

Serves 4 to 5

¾ cup brown or green lentils, rinsed (see page 39)

Salt

1 tablespoon olive oil

1 medium yellow onion, diced

3 garlic cloves, minced

½ jalapeño, seeded and minced

2 large tomatoes, diced

2 teaspoons chili powder

½ teaspoon smoked paprika

¼ teaspoon chipotle powder

¼ teaspoon ground mustard seed

1 tablespoon tomato paste

1½ cups frozen corn kernels

2 tablespoons chopped fresh cilantro

Freshly ground black pepper

Freshly squeezed lime juice

Place the lentils in a medium saucepan with 3½ cups water and a pinch of salt. Bring the water to a boil. Reduce the heat to a gentle simmer and cook the lentils for about 15 minutes, or until al dente. (Avoid overcooking the lentils or they will become mushy.) Drain the cooked lentils. Set aside.

Meanwhile, heat the olive oil in a large skillet over medium heat. Add the onion and sauté for about 5 minutes, or until translucent. Add the garlic and jalapeño and cook for about another 30 seconds, or until fragrant.

Add the tomatoes and continue cooking for about 7 minutes, or until the water from the tomatoes evaporates and they start to stick to the bottom of the skillet. Add the chili powder, smoked paprika, chipotle powder, and ground mustard and cook for 1 minute more. Add the tomato paste and cook for another 30 seconds, stirring constantly. Mix in 1 cup water.

Use an immersion blender to blend the sauce until smooth. (Alternatively, you can transfer the sauce to a blender.)

Continue cooking the sauce over medium-low heat and add the lentils and corn. Simmer for 5 minutes, adding more water as needed until the desired consistency. Stir in the cilantro. Add salt, pepper, and lime juice to taste.

Fire-Roasted Tempeh Chili

1 (8-ounce) package **tempeh**

Marinade

1 tablespoon **olive oil**

2 teaspoons **low-sodium tamari or soy sauce**

¾ teaspoon **chili powder**

¾ teaspoon **smoked paprika**

¼ teaspoon **chipotle powder**

¼ teaspoon **garlic powder**

Chili

1 tablespoon **olive oil**

1 large **yellow onion**, diced

3 **garlic cloves**, minced

1½ teaspoons **smoked paprika**

1½ teaspoons **ground cumin**

¾ teaspoon **chili powder**

¼ teaspoon **chipotle powder**

2 tablespoons **tomato paste**

1 (14.5-ounce) can **fire-roasted or diced tomatoes**

1 (15-ounce) can **black beans**, undrained, or 1½ cups cooked beans plus ½ cup cooking liquid

1 teaspoon **maple syrup**

¾ cup **frozen corn** kernels

Vegetable broth or water (optional)

2 tablespoons chopped **fresh cilantro**

Freshly squeezed lime juice

Salt

I recently invited four friends over for dinner, all of whom I had a standing joke with about how much they despise tempeh. I figured they would be the ultimate test of this recipe. They devoured it, asked for seconds, and then insisted I give them the recipe.

Simmering your tempeh prior to use is optional, but I highly recommend taking this extra step, as it removes any bitterness from the tempeh.

Serves 3 to 4

In a medium saucepan, bring enough water to cover the tempeh by about 2 inches to a boil. Add the tempeh, reduce the heat, and simmer for 3 minutes. Drain the tempeh and pat it dry. Set aside to cool.

Meanwhile, prepare the marinade: In a medium bowl, mix the olive oil, tamari, chili powder, smoked paprika, chipotle powder, and garlic powder to blend.

Use your hands to break up the tempeh into small crumbles (see page 37). Transfer the crumbles to the bowl with the marinade and use your hands to rub the marinade on the tempeh until all the crumbles are well coated.

In a large nonstick skillet over medium heat, sauté the crumbles for about 7 minutes, or until golden brown and slightly crispy. Set aside.

Make the chili: In a medium saucepan, heat the olive oil over medium heat. Sauté the onion for about 5 minutes, or until translucent. Add the garlic and cook for 30 seconds. Add the smoked paprika, cumin, chili powder, and chipotle powder and cook for 1 minute more. Stir in the tomato paste and cook for 1 more minute, stirring constantly. Mix in the canned tomatoes. (If desired, use an immersion blender or blender and process until about half of the sauce is smooth.)

Add the beans and their liquid, ¾ cup water, the maple syrup, corn, and tempeh crumbles. Stir to incorporate. Simmer for about 5 minutes, or until everything is warmed through, adding vegetable broth or water as needed for the desired consistency.

Stir in the chopped cilantro and add lime juice and salt to taste.

Mushroom Chili

1 tablespoon **olive oil**

1 medium **yellow onion**, diced

3 **garlic cloves**, minced

1 small **jalapeño**, seeded and minced

1 teaspoon **dried oregano**

¾ teaspoon **chili powder**

¾ teaspoon **smoked paprika**

¾ teaspoon **ground cumin**

½ teaspoon **ground coriander**

1 (8-ounce) package **baby bella (cremini) or white button mushrooms**, stems trimmed, roughly chopped

2 medium **carrots**, diced (¾ cup)

1½ tablespoons **tomato paste**

Salt

1 (14.5-ounce) can **diced tomatoes**

1½ cups **vegetable broth**

1 (15-ounce) can **black beans**, drained and rinsed, or 1½ cups cooked beans

1 teaspoon **mellow (white) miso**

1 tablespoon **low-sodium tamari or soy sauce**

1 teaspoon **freshly squeezed lime juice**

1 cup finely chopped **kale leaves** (mid-ribs removed) (optional)

Freshly ground black pepper to taste

The umami quality of mushrooms and their meaty texture make them a well-suited ingredient for chilis. In addition to the usual chili spices, I added miso and tamari here to complement the mushroom flavor. It turns out that this combination rocks! And because of the Asian-inspired twist, this chili also pairs deliciously with noodles.

Make sure to fully dissolve your miso in water before adding it to the chili. It's not pleasant to bite into chunks of miso!

Serves 4

Heat the olive oil in a large saucepan or Dutch oven over medium heat. Add the onion and cook for about 5 minutes, or until softened. Add the garlic, jalapeño, oregano, chili powder, smoked paprika, cumin, and coriander. Cook for 30 seconds, stirring constantly.

Mix in the mushrooms, carrots, tomato paste, and ¼ teaspoon salt and cook for 2 minutes more.

Add the diced tomatoes and vegetable broth and bring to a boil. Reduce the heat, cover, and simmer for 5 minutes.

Stir in the beans and simmer, uncovered, for about 7 minutes, or until the sauce has thickened to the desired consistency. (While cooking, mash some of the beans using a spatula or potato masher to thicken the sauce, if desired.)

In a small bowl, stir the miso into 1 tablespoon warm water until completely dissolved.

Add the dissolved miso, tamari, and lime juice to the beans and stir well to combine. Mix in the kale (if using) and cook for about 2 minutes more, or until the kale is just wilted.

Season with salt and pepper.

Practically Vegan

Potato Bean Chili

2 tablespoons olive oil

1 large yellow onion, diced

1 medium red bell pepper, chopped (about 1 cup)

1 pound baby yellow or Yukon Gold potatoes, cut into ½-inch pieces (about 3 cups)

3 garlic cloves, minced

2 teaspoons chili powder

1 teaspoon paprika

1 teaspoon dried oregano

½ teaspoon ground cumin

¼ cup plus 1 tablespoon tomato paste

1 (14.5-ounce) can diced tomatoes

1 (15-ounce) can pinto beans, drained and rinsed, or 1½ cups cooked beans

2 tablespoons chopped fresh cilantro

Salt and freshly ground black pepper to taste

Potatoes are the ultimate comfort food. Chili is also high up on the list. And so, friends, you can only imagine how much comfort this potato chili is going to bring you! It's also a very pantry-friendly recipe. Almost any type of bean will work. I usually use pinto beans, but black beans, kidney beans, black-eyed peas, chickpeas (technically a legume), and most other beans would also be delicious.

Serves 4 to 5

Heat the olive oil in a large saucepan or Dutch oven over medium heat. Add the onion, bell pepper, and potatoes and cook for about 5 minutes, or until the onion is translucent, stirring frequently.

Add the garlic, chili powder, paprika, oregano, and cumin, stir, and cook for 1 more minute. Add the tomato paste and cook for 1 minute more, stirring constantly.

Mix in the diced tomatoes and beans and bring to a boil. Reduce the heat, cover, and simmer for about 30 minutes, or until the potatoes are fork-tender. Stir frequently and add water as needed if the chili becomes too dry.

Mix in the cilantro. Season with salt and pepper.

Peanut Pinto Chili

1 tablespoon **olive oil**

1 medium **yellow onion**, diced

4 **garlic cloves**, minced

1 **jalapeño**, seeded and minced

1 teaspoon **chili powder**

1 teaspoon **ground cumin**

1 teaspoon **paprika**

¼ teaspoon **cayenne pepper**

3 tablespoons **tomato paste**

1 medium **sweet potato**, peeled and cut into 1-inch pieces (about 2 cups)

4 cups **vegetable broth**

½ cup **creamy peanut butter or almond butter**

1 tablespoon **low-sodium tamari or soy sauce**

1 (15-ounce) can **pinto beans or chickpeas**, drained and rinsed, or 1½ cups cooked beans

2 cups chopped **kale leaves**

2 teaspoons **freshly squeezed lime juice**

Salt to taste

2 tablespoons chopped **fresh cilantro**, for garnish

2 tablespoons **chopped peanuts**, for garnish

Lime wedges, for serving

Adding nut butter is a nutritious and scrumptious way to thicken a sauce, chili, stew, or curry. Not only do you get the added nutritional benefit of heart-healthy fats and some extra plant-based protein, but you also get a creamier, more satisfying dish. Most nut butters will work for this recipe. In addition to peanut butter, almond and cashew butters are my other favorites. But then I would have to change the name of the dish!

Serves 4 to 5

Heat the olive oil in a large saucepan over medium heat. Add the onion and cook for about 5 minutes, or until translucent. Add the garlic and jalapeño and cook for another 30 seconds. Add the chili powder, cumin, paprika, and cayenne and cook for 1 minute more. Add the tomato paste and cook for 1 more minute, stirring constantly.

Mix in the sweet potato, vegetable broth, peanut butter, and tamari and stir to combine. Bring the broth to a boil, then reduce the heat and simmer for about 12 minutes, or until the sweet potato is just fork-tender.

Add the beans and kale. Cook until the kale is just wilted and the beans are warmed through. Add the lime juice and salt to taste.

Garnish with cilantro and chopped peanuts. Serve with lime wedges.

Chapter 3

Curry

In addition to being of Indian descent, I grew up in Jamaica and England—all three arguably in the ten top countries for curry—so it should come as no surprise that curry is one of my favorite foods.

Curries are typically served with rice or naan so as not to distract from the main event. They also pair well with noodles, especially Thai-inspired curries. Explore serving yours with different sides to see what tickles your fancy.

Red Lentil Go-To Curry

2 cups **red lentils**, rinsed (see page 39)

1 tablespoon **neutral cooking oil** (see page 18)

1 medium **yellow onion**, diced large

4 **garlic cloves**, minced

1 tablespoon grated **fresh ginger**

2 medium **carrots**, cut into ¼-inch-thick rounds

1 tablespoon **curry powder**

½ teaspoon **garam masala**

¼ teaspoon **ground turmeric**

1 tablespoon **mirin or maple syrup**

1 tablespoon **tomato paste**

2 tablespoons **low-sodium tamari or soy sauce**

2 cups **vegetable broth**

Salt and freshly ground black pepper to taste

3 tablespoons chopped **fresh cilantro**, for garnish

Red lentils are my go-to when I forget to soak my beans, or if I have very little time to put dinner on the table. They cook very quickly, which is a blessing when you have hangry kids! In fact, if they are really hangry, my teens will make this curry themselves. It's that easy. (I may have to grate the ginger, but that's about it.)

Red lentils are an awesome source of plant-based protein, and they're very versatile. I use them in curries, burgers, pasta sauces, sloppy joes . . . the list goes on.

Serves 4

In a small saucepan, add the lentils with enough water to cover by about 1 inch. Bring the water to a boil. Reduce the heat and gently simmer the lentils for about 10 minutes, or until they are cooked but still firm (al dente), adding more water as needed to keep them covered. Drain and set aside.

Heat the oil in a medium saucepan over medium heat. Add the onion and cook for about 5 minutes, or until golden brown. Add the garlic, ginger, and carrots and cook for 1 minute more. Add the curry powder, garam masala, turmeric, mirin, tomato paste, tamari, and vegetable broth. Cover and simmer for about 10 minutes, or until the carrots are tender.

Use an immersion blender or a standard blender to puree the mixture until smooth.

Add the lentils to the sauce and cook until just warmed through. Season with salt and pepper and garnish with cilantro.

Thai Veggie Curry with Tofu

If you ever want to impress a dinner guest, this attractive curry might be the dish for doing so. The red from the curry paste is so vibrant, and the mushrooms rise to the surface and glisten on the red backdrop. (Clearly, I'm fascinated by food!) It's also one of the quickest curries to make, so your guests will be doubly impressed by how skillful you are in the kitchen.

The recipe for this curry can be used as a base for other veggies, too. You can swap out the mushrooms and peppers and use whatever you have on hand. Just stick to the approximate quantities in the recipe. I added tofu for protein, but you can leave it out or substitute the tofu with either chickpeas or tempeh.

Serves 4

1 tablespoon neutral cooking oil (see page 18)

1 small yellow onion, diced

3 garlic cloves, minced

2 teaspoons minced fresh ginger

1 large red bell pepper, thinly sliced

2 tablespoons Thai red curry paste

1 (8-ounce) package baby bella (cremini) or white button mushrooms, stems trimmed

1 (14-ounce) can unsweetened coconut milk

½ (14-ounce) block extra-firm tofu (optional), pressed and cut into ¾-inch cubes (see page 34)

1½ tablespoons low-sodium soy sauce or tamari, plus more to taste

1 teaspoon maple syrup, plus more to taste

2 teaspoons freshly squeezed lime juice, plus more to taste

Salt to taste

Noodles (optional)

Heat the oil in a large saucepan over medium heat. Add the onion and cook for about 5 minutes, or until translucent. Add the garlic and ginger and cook for 30 seconds more. Add the bell pepper and cook for about 3 minutes, or until just tender. Mix in the red curry paste and cook for 1 minute, stirring constantly.

Add the mushrooms and coconut milk and stir to combine. Simmer for about 10 minutes, or until the mushrooms are just tender.

Add the tofu (if using), soy sauce, and maple syrup. Add up to ⅓ cup water, if needed, for a thinner curry, according to your taste. Simmer for about 3 minutes, or until the tofu is warmed through.

Add the lime juice and salt. If desired, adjust the soy sauce, maple syrup, and lime to taste and serve with noodles, if desired.

Simple Chickpea Masala

3 tablespoons **neutral cooking oil** (see page 18)

¼ teaspoon **cumin seeds**

¼ teaspoon **brown mustard seeds**

1 medium **yellow onion**, finely diced

2 teaspoons **ground coriander**

1 teaspoon **ground cumin**

¼ teaspoon **ground turmeric**

⅛ teaspoon **cayenne pepper**

⅛ teaspoon **finely ground black pepper**

1 (14.5-ounce) can **diced tomatoes**

4 cups **cooked chickpeas**, or about 2½ (15-ounce) cans chickpeas, drained and rinsed

1 (14-ounce) can **unsweetened coconut cream**, or to taste (optional)

1 teaspoon **salt**, or to taste

1 teaspoon **freshly squeezed lemon juice**, or to taste

2 tablespoons chopped **fresh cilantro**

Cashew yogurt or Yogurt Drizzle Sauce (page 255), for serving (optional)

You can't go wrong with this simple, flavorful dish. The recipe uses both cumin seeds and brown mustard seeds, as well as a blend of pantry-friendly spices to flavor the oil. Don't forget to smell your fragrant oil, as this will let you know when it's ready for your onions.

This recipe calls for coconut cream, which is different from coconut milk. While the two are made from the same ingredients, coconut cream has a higher fat content, making it more creamy and less watered down. It's an optional ingredient as the recipe is still very tasty without it. But I highly recommend adding some as it gives this dish a richer flavor and adds body, as well as enhances the color. We eat with our eyes first, remember!

You can substitute 1½ cups dried brown or green lentils for the chickpeas, but you will need to add more water as the lentils cook. Keep cooking your masala and adding water until the lentils are tender.

Serves 3

Heat the oil in a medium skillet over medium heat. Add the cumin seeds and brown mustard seeds and cook for about 1 minute, or until the mustard seeds either begin to pop or turn a grayish color. Stir constantly.

Add the onion and cook for about 5 minutes, until softened. Add the coriander, ground cumin, turmeric, cayenne, and black pepper and cook for about 30 seconds more, or until fragrant, stirring constantly. Add the tomatoes and cook for 1 minute.

Stir in the chickpeas and ½ cup water. Cover and simmer for 10 minutes. Use a potato masher or the side of a spatula to partially mash about a third of the chickpeas to add some texture to the sauce. Add the coconut cream (if using), 2 tablespoons at a time, until the desired texture. Mix well to combine.

Stir in the salt, lemon juice, and cilantro. If desired, serve with cashew yogurt or yogurt drizzle sauce.

Butternut Squash Tahini Curry

This curry gets its creamy texture by combining blended butternut squash with tahini. Vegan curries often use coconut milk or cashews for creaminess, but I like exploring other options as there's only so much coconut milk and cashews one can consume. This combo of blended squash and tahini works perfectly. It's so yummy, friends.

Honeynut squash is my first choice for this curry as it tends to be very sweet, but it can be tricky to find. Butternut squash is more readily available and also super delicious, but you might want to add a tad more maple syrup if you prefer a sweeter curry.

To add more protein to this dish I mixed in Chickpea Croutons (page 222) during the final stages of cooking. Or you can add Crispy Baked Tofu Cubes (page 213) or plain chickpeas as desired.

Serves 2 to 3

1 tablespoon olive oil

1 small yellow onion, diced small

1 tablespoon grated fresh ginger

4 garlic cloves, minced

1 small red chili pepper, seeded and minced

1 large red bell pepper, cut into ¾-inch pieces

1 medium butternut squash or honeynut squash, peeled and cut into ¾-inch cubes (3½ cups)

2½ tablespoons Thai red curry paste

3 cups vegetable broth, plus more as needed

3 tablespoons tahini

1 tablespoon low-sodium soy sauce or tamari

1 tablespoon freshly squeezed lime juice, plus more to taste

½ teaspoon maple syrup, or to taste

Chickpea Croutons (page 222), (optional)

Salt to taste

¼ cup chopped fresh cilantro, for garnish

Heat the olive oil in a large saucepan or Dutch oven over medium heat. Add the onion and cook for about 5 minutes, or until translucent. Add the ginger, garlic, and chili pepper and cook for 30 seconds more.

Add the bell pepper and cook for 30 seconds. Mix in the butternut squash and cook for 1 minute more, stirring frequently. Add the red curry paste and cook for 1 more minute, stirring constantly.

Stir in the vegetable broth and bring to a gentle boil. Reduce the heat to a vigorous simmer and cook, covered, for about 5 minutes, or until the squash is tender.

Transfer half of the butternut squash and the liquid to a blender. (Be careful not to transfer the bell pepper pieces.) Blend on high until smooth (see page 40 on how to blend hot liquid). Return the blended squash and liquid to the saucepan with the remaining curry, stirring to combine.

Stir in the tahini, soy sauce, lime juice, and maple syrup.

Mix in some chickpea croutons, if using. Add more vegetable broth, depending on the desired consistency. Cook over low heat until warmed through.

Season with salt and adjust the lime juice and maple syrup to taste. Garnish with cilantro.

Practically Vegan

Black Lentil Coconut Masala

3 tablespoons **neutral cooking oil** (see page 18)

¼ teaspoon **brown mustard seeds**

¼ teaspoon **cumin seeds**

1 large **yellow onion**, finely diced

2 teaspoons **ground coriander**

1 teaspoon **ground cumin**

¼ teaspoon **ground turmeric**

⅛ teaspoon **cayenne pepper**

⅛ teaspoon **finely ground black pepper**

1½ cups **dried black lentils**, rinsed (see page 39)

3½ cups **vegetable broth**, plus more as needed

1 (14.5-ounce) can **diced tomatoes**

1 (14-ounce) can **unsweetened coconut milk**, or to taste

1 teaspoon **salt**, or to taste

2 tablespoons chopped **fresh cilantro**, for garnish

This recipe is a variation of Simple Chickpea Masala (page 100). It uses the same spices, but instead of chickpeas, it calls for black lentils, which are cooked in the curry itself for even more depth of flavor. This curry is also a thinner consistency as it uses coconut milk in place of coconut cream.

Black lentils, also known as Beluga lentils, are small and dark. Unlike brown and red lentils, they hold their shape indefinitely when cooked, giving this dish even more texture. The coconut milk is added towards the end for a delicious sweet and nutty flavor and for creaminess.

Take note, my culinary chemists: In this recipe the tomatoes are added once the lentils are fully cooked and not before. This is because the acidity in tomatoes can make it harder for lentils to cook, therefore increasing the cooking time. This is the same for beans. In fact, too much acid can prevent beans from ever becoming tender. I've made this mistake!

Serves 5

Heat the oil in a medium skillet over medium heat. Add the brown mustard seeds and cumin seeds and cook for about 1 minute, or until the mustard seeds either turn a grayish color or begin to pop, stirring constantly.

Add the onion and cook for about 5 minutes, or until softened. Add the coriander, ground cumin, turmeric, cayenne, and black pepper and cook for about 30 seconds more, or until fragrant, stirring constantly.

Stir in the lentils and vegetable broth. Bring the liquid to a boil, then reduce the heat to a simmer. Cover and cook for about 15 minutes, or until the lentils are tender, stirring occasionally. Add more broth or water, as needed, to keep the lentils covered.

Once the lentils are cooked, stir in the diced tomatoes and cook for 5 minutes. Stir in the coconut milk to taste, adding one quarter cup at a time. Simmer for about 1 minute more, or until warmed through. Season with salt and garnish with cilantro.

Cauliflower–Sweet Potato Curry

2 tablespoons olive oil

1 medium yellow onion, diced

3 garlic cloves, minced

2 teaspoons minced fresh ginger

2 tablespoons curry powder

¾ teaspoon ground cumin

¾ teaspoon ground coriander

½ teaspoon ground turmeric

1 large sweet potato, peeled and cut into 1-inch pieces (about 3 cups)

¼ cup tomato paste

1 (14.5-ounce) can diced tomatoes

2 cups vegetable broth

1 medium head cauliflower, cut into 1½-inch florets (about 2½ cups)

1 (14-ounce) can unsweetened coconut milk

Salt to taste

¼ cup chopped peanuts or raw cashews (optional)

2 tablespoons chopped fresh cilantro, for garnish

Sneaking sweet potato into curries is one of my go-to tricks, because even sweet-potato haters don't know it's there. (Is there even such a thing as a sweet-potato hater?) It makes the curry even more nutritious by adding resistant starch that feeds our friendly gut bacteria, fiber that makes us feel full so we don't overeat, and several vitamins and minerals.

Visually, it turns the curry a gorgeous hue of orange, and as the saying goes, we eat with our eyes first. It also gives the curry a smooth texture, making it even creamier.

Serves 4 to 5

Heat the olive oil in a large saucepan over medium heat. Add the onion and cook for about 5 minutes, or until translucent.

Stir in the garlic, ginger, curry powder, cumin, coriander, and turmeric. Cook for 1 minute more.

Add the sweet potato and tomato paste. Cook for 1 more minute, stirring constantly, so that the sweet potato is coated with the spices.

Add the diced tomatoes, vegetable broth, and cauliflower and stir. Bring to a boil, then reduce the heat. Cover and simmer the curry for about 20 minutes, or until the sweet potato is fork-tender. Stir frequently while checking for doneness.

Mix in the coconut milk. Cook for about 2 minutes more, or until everything is warmed through. Season with salt, mix in the peanuts (if using), and garnish with cilantro.

Creamy Dal

1 tablespoon **neutral cooking oil** (see page 18)

1 large **yellow onion**, diced

5 **garlic cloves**, minced

1 tablespoon minced **fresh ginger**

2 small **green chilies, or** 1 **jalapeño**, minced, or to taste

1 tablespoon **curry powder**

1 teaspoon **garam masala**

1 teaspoon **ground mustard seed**

1 teaspoon **ground coriander**

½ teaspoon **ground cumin**

¼ teaspoon **ground turmeric**

2 large **tomatoes**, diced (about 1¾ cups)

2 cups **red lentils**, rinsed (see page 39)

4½ cups **vegetable broth**, plus more as needed

⅓ cup **raw cashews** (optional), soaked, drained, and rinsed (see page 39)

Salt to taste

Freshly squeezed lime juice to taste

2 to 3 tablespoons chopped **fresh cilantro**, for garnish

Coconut yogurt or Yogurt Drizzle Sauce (page 255), for serving (optional)

Dal is both an ingredient and a dish. It's a collective term for dried split pulses (lentils, beans, and peas), as well as a soup or thick stew. Packed with fiber and protein, inexpensive to make, and luxurious to eat, Dal is the ultimate in plant-based ingredients—or dishes!

Red lentils cook much more quickly than most other pulses, which is why it's my go-to for making last-minute dal.

Blending soaked cashews with cooked dal makes it extra creamy and comforting. But there's also the option to go nut-free. Simply blend without adding the cashews. Both versions are equally delicious.

To reduce the spice in this recipe, seed the green chilies (or jalapeño) before mincing. You can also reduce the number of green chilies in the recipe.

Serves 5

Heat the oil in a large saucepan or Dutch oven over medium heat. Add the onion and cook for 8 to 10 minutes, until golden brown. Stir in the garlic, ginger, and green chilies and cook for 30 seconds more. Add the curry powder, garam masala, ground mustard, coriander, cumin, and turmeric and cook for another 30 seconds, stirring constantly. Add the tomatoes and cook for about 10 minutes, or until they become dry and start sticking to the bottom of the saucepan, stirring frequently.

Add the lentils and 4 cups of the vegetable broth, stir, and bring to a gentle boil. Reduce the heat to low, cover, and simmer for about 15 minutes, or until the lentils are tender. Stir occasionally, adding more broth as needed to keep the lentils covered.

Transfer 1 cup of the dal to a high-speed blender, along with the remaining ½ cup vegetable broth. Add the cashews (if using). Blend on high until smooth. (See page 40 on how to blend hot liquid.) Return the blended dal to the saucepan with the remaining dal. Mix to incorporate. Cook over low heat for about 3 minutes, or until the dal is warmed through, stirring frequently. Add more vegetable broth or water as needed until the desired consistency.

Add salt and lime juice to taste. Garnish with cilantro. If desired, serve with coconut yogurt or yogurt drizzle sauce.

Tofu Curry

Baked Tofu

1 (14-ounce) block **extra-firm tofu**, pressed and cut into ¾-inch cubes (see page 34)

1 tablespoon **cornstarch**

½ teaspoon **garlic powder**

¼ teaspoon **salt**

Curry

1 tablespoon **neutral cooking oil** (see page 18)

1 medium **yellow onion**, diced

3 **garlic cloves**, minced

2 teaspoons minced **fresh ginger**

1¾ teaspoons **curry powder**

1¼ teaspoons **garam masala**

¾ teaspoon **ground cumin**

½ teaspoon **ground coriander**

½ teaspoon **ground turmeric**

2 tablespoons **tomato paste**

1 (14.5-ounce) can **crushed tomatoes**

1 (14-ounce) can **unsweetened coconut milk**

⅛ teaspoon **finely ground black pepper**

Salt

2 tablespoons chopped **fresh cilantro**, for garnish

One of my favorite ways to eat tofu is in a flavorful curry. This one's a breeze to put together and a pleasure to eat. If you like your tofu on the crispier side, follow the recipe and bake your tofu before adding it to the curry. Otherwise, if you are short on time or prefer tofu with a softer texture, you can skip this step and start with sautéing your onions.

This curry is big on spices, giving it lots of flavor. You'll be glad you followed my advice and bought all those spices in the pantry list—or you'll be regretting you didn't!

Coconut milk is ideal for balancing the spices in this curry. But if you're not a fan or don't have any in your pantry, you can substitute oat milk or another plant-based milk.

Serves 4

Bake the tofu: Preheat the oven to 400°F. Line a baking sheet with parchment paper or a silicone mat.

Place the tofu into a large plastic zip-top bag or an airtight container. In a small bowl, combine the cornstarch, garlic powder, and salt and mix well. Add the cornstarch mixture to the plastic bag and gently rotate the bag, moving the tofu around until all the pieces are coated with the cornstarch mixture.

Transfer the tofu to the prepared baking sheet. Spread the tofu cubes in an even layer so that none are touching. Bake for 7 minutes, then flip them over. Bake for about 7 minutes more, or until the cubes are golden brown. Remove from the oven and set aside.

Make the curry: While the tofu is baking, heat the oil in a large saucepan over medium heat. Add the onion and cook for about 5 minutes, or until translucent. Add the garlic and ginger and cook for about 30 seconds, or until fragrant. Stir in the curry powder, garam masala, cumin, coriander, and turmeric and cook for 1 minute more. Mix in the tomato paste and cook for another 1 minute, stirring constantly.

Add the crushed tomatoes and coconut milk. Bring to a gentle boil. Reduce the heat and simmer for about 3 minutes, or until warmed through. Stir in the tofu and cook for about 2 minutes more, or until the tofu is warm.

Stir in the black pepper, season with salt, and garnish with cilantro.

Creamy Thai Red Curry

2 tablespoons **neutral cooking oil** (see page 18)

1 large **yellow onion**, diced

1 medium **sweet potato**, peeled and cut into 1-inch pieces (about 2 cups)

3 large **garlic cloves**, minced

1 tablespoon minced **fresh ginger**

2 tablespoons **Thai red curry paste**

1½ tablespoons **low-sodium tamari or soy sauce**

1 (14-ounce) can **unsweetened coconut milk**

1½ cups **red lentils**, rinsed (see page 39)

3 cups **vegetable broth**, plus more as needed

2 tablespoons **freshly squeezed lime juice**

1 cup **fresh basil leaves**, roughly chopped

Salt to taste

2 **limes**, sliced into wedges, for serving

I'll let you in on a little secret that I didn't tell my editor, as I was allowed only a certain number of recipes in the book. This is actually two recipes disguised as one. The blended puree can be enjoyed as a most delicious sweet potato soup. You can stop the recipe after blending the sauce. No need to add any lentils. Just mix a little vegetable broth into the puree for your desired consistency and you have the best sweet potato soup ever.

Another practical thing about this recipe is you need only one pot to make it, which means whoever is on dish duty better be pretty darn grateful!

The coconut milk does a fantastic job of melding the flavors together, but it can be subbed with any plant-based milk. Oat milk is an especially good option.

Serves 5

Heat the oil in a large saucepan over medium-high heat. Add the onion and sweet potato and cook for 5 to 7 minutes, until the onion turns translucent. Add the garlic and ginger and cook for about 30 seconds more, or until fragrant. Add the red curry paste and cook for 1 minute more, stirring constantly.

Add the tamari and coconut milk. Bring to a gentle boil, then reduce the heat. Cover and simmer for about 15 minutes or until the sweet potato is fork-tender, stirring frequently.

Using an immersion blender or a standard blender, puree the mixture until smooth, then return it to the saucepan.

Add the red lentils and the vegetable broth to the saucepan with the blended sauce and bring to a gentle boil. Reduce the heat to a gentle simmer, cover, and cook for about 15 minutes, or until the lentils are tender. Stir frequently and add more broth or water as needed to keep the lentils submerged. Once the lentils are cooked, add more broth or water until the desired consistency.

Stir in the lime juice and fresh basil. Season with salt. Serve with lime wedges.

Chapter 4

Burgers & Patties

Stuff It, Wrap It, Top It

Here you'll find burgers and patties, and other recipes where something gets either wrapped, stuffed, or topped—hence the long title of this chapter. I like to think of these as my fun recipes, ones that inspire your inner creativity. Come up with your own ways to stuff, wrap, and top, and have a blast.

Patties versus *burgers*—are these two words interchangeable? I find these terms so confusing, but for the purposes of this book, I refer to "patties" as the disks that go inside split buns or rolls with various condiments and toppings to make burgers. Now that we've cleared up any confusion around terminology, go ahead and turn these patties into delicious burgers by serving them in warm and toasty buns loaded with your choice of add-ons. Or drop the bun altogether and serve your patties with a side salad, veggies, or potatoes. There are no rules here.

If you do choose to eat your patty in a bun, I highly recommend warming your buns before serving. Preheat the oven to 350°F and toast the buns for about 5 minutes, or until they are warmed through and lightly crispy. (You can also use a toaster oven.) Remove the warm buns from the oven and place them into a basket or bowl with a tea towel on top, or wrap them in aluminum foil to keep them from becoming hard and crunchy.

For cheeseburgers, place sliced vegan cheese on the patties for 3 to 4 minutes in the oven before they finish cooking so the cheese can melt.

Try the recipes from the Dips, Dressings & Sauces chapter (pages 249–265) with these patties and burgers to decide which combinations you like most.

Smoky Lentil Burgers

2 tablespoons **flax meal** (ground flaxseeds)

1 cup **green or brown lentils**, rinsed (see page 39)

¾ cup **panko bread crumbs**

2 tablespoons **olive oil**

1½ teaspoons **vegan Worcestershire sauce**

1 teaspoon **low-sodium tamari or soy sauce**

½ teaspoon **garlic powder**

½ teaspoon **onion powder**

½ teaspoon **smoked paprika**

¼ teaspoon **chipotle powder**

¼ teaspoon **finely ground black pepper**

Salt

Serving (Optional)

4 **burger buns**, toasted (see opposite page)

1 medium **yellow onion**, sliced and caramelized, **or** 1 medium **red onion**, thinly sliced

2 **avocados**, sliced

Aioli (page 254)

Vegan patty recipes can get quite convoluted sometimes. I remember reading one burger recipe that instructed, "Sauté enough to remove all moisture to ensure you have a more cohesive/less bread crumb/ binder to mix." Hmmm?

Anyway, I'm keeping things simple with this one. I don't want y'all to get your knickers in a twist from making burgers. There are a million other reasons to get your knickers in a twist, but burgers shouldn't be one of them.

Enjoy these protein-packed patties with whatever add-ons and condiments you're in the mood for. They're very versatile.

Serves 4 (makes 4 patties)

Preheat the oven to 375°F. Line a baking sheet with parchment paper or a silicone mat. Set aside.

In a small bowl, make the "flax egg" by mixing the flax meal with 3 tablespoons water. Set aside.

In a medium saucepan, combine the lentils with 3 cups water. Bring to a boil, then reduce the heat. Simmer, uncovered, for about 15 minutes, or until the lentils are al dente. Add more water as needed to keep the lentils submerged. Drain the cooked lentils and rinse them under cold water.

Transfer the lentils to a large bowl and partially mash them using a potato masher. The mixture should be chunky with some whole lentils remaining. To the bowl, add the panko, olive oil, Worcestershire, tamari, garlic powder, onion powder, smoked paprika, chipotle, black pepper, ¼ teaspoon salt, and the flax egg. First mix the ingredients with a large spoon, then use your hands to fully incorporate everything. Taste the mixture and add more salt to taste, if necessary.

Using ¾ cup of the mixture for each patty and your hands, shape 4 patties into disks. Place them on the prepared baking sheet. Bake for 15 minutes before flipping them over. Bake for another 10 minutes, or until firm and lightly golden.

To serve: If desired, serve the patties on toasted buns with your choice of garnishes and condiments.

"I Can't Believe It's Tofu" Burgers

This is one of my favorite burgers. They require a bit more effort to make, but it's well worth it. Just like all the best things in life.

These are full of umami flavor, which gives them a meaty quality, and the texture is just like what a good burger's should be. Honestly, I can quite comfortably eat two of these burgers in one sitting, so depending on how hungry you are, this recipe may only serve three.

Serves 6 (makes 6 patties)

1½ cups **walnuts**

1 tablespoon **nutritional yeast**

1 teaspoon **dried oregano**

¾ teaspoon **smoked paprika**

¾ teaspoon **garlic powder**

¾ teaspoon **onion powder**

½ teaspoon **ground cumin**

¼ teaspoon **cayenne pepper**

2 tablespoons **low-sodium soy sauce or tamari**

2 tablespoons **tomato paste**

2 tablespoons **olive oil**

1 tablespoon **maple syrup**

1 (14-ounce) block **extra-firm tofu**, pressed and crumbled (see page 34)

1 small **yellow onion, or 2 shallots**, finely diced (about ½ cup)

3 tablespoons **chia seeds**

¼ cup **old-fashioned rolled oats or store-bought oat flour**

1 tablespoon **vegan Worcestershire sauce**

¾ teaspoon **salt**, or to taste

In a food processor, pulse the walnuts until coarsely ground. (Be careful not to overdo it. You do not want the walnuts to become flour.) Set aside.

In a large bowl, mix together the nutritional yeast, oregano, smoked paprika, garlic powder, onion powder, cumin, cayenne, soy sauce, tomato paste, 1 tablespoon of the olive oil, and the maple syrup. Add the tofu crumbles and chopped walnuts. Use your hands to rub the spice mixture onto the tofu and walnuts until they are evenly coated.

Heat the remaining 1 tablespoon olive oil in a large nonstick skillet over medium-high heat. Add the onion and cook for about 3 minutes, or until translucent. Add the tofu-walnut mixture and 1 tablespoon water, stir, and cook for about 7 minutes, or until the mixture browns and becomes dry.

Transfer the tofu-walnut mixture to a large bowl. Set aside.

Preheat the oven to 375°F. Line a baking sheet with parchment paper or a silicone mat. Set aside.

In a small bowl, make a "chia egg" by combining the chia seeds with 4½ tablespoons water. Stir to combine. Leave to set for at least 5 minutes.

Pulse the rolled oats in a food processor until they turn into a flour-like consistency. (Skip this step if using store-bought oat flour.)

Add the chia egg and oat flour to the tofu-walnut mixture. Add the Worcestershire sauce and use your hands to fully incorporate the ingredients. Add salt to taste and mix again.

Serving (Optional)

6 **burger buns**, toasted
  (see page 112)

6 slices **vegan cheese**

2 medium **tomatoes**, sliced

2 heaping cups **chopped lettuce**

Ketchup, store-bought or
  homemade (page 265)

Vegan mayonnaise

Mustard

Form 6 patties using about ½ cup of the mixture for each; they should be about 1-inch thick. Transfer the patties to the prepared baking sheet. Bake for 15 minutes before flipping them over. Bake for about 15 minutes more, or until slightly crispy on the outside. Transfer the patties to a cooling rack and allow to sit for 5 minutes after baking to firm up.

To serve: If desired, serve the patties on toasted buns with your choice of garnishes and condiments.

Black Bean Corn Burgers

1 tablespoon olive oil

1 small yellow onion, chopped (about ½ cup)

3 garlic cloves, minced

1 small jalapeño, seeded and minced

1 teaspoon dried oregano

¾ teaspoon smoked paprika

½ teaspoon ground cumin

½ teaspoon garlic powder

½ teaspoon chili powder

Salt

1 (15-ounce) can black beans, drained and rinsed, or 1½ cups cooked black beans

1 cup frozen sweet corn kernels, thawed and drained

1 tablespoon vegan Worcestershire sauce

1 tablespoon freshly squeezed lime juice

½ cup all-purpose, whole-wheat, or gluten-free flour

½ cup dried bread crumbs

¼ teaspoon finely ground black pepper

1 tablespoon chopped fresh cilantro

Serving (Optional)

5 burger buns, toasted (see page 112)

2 medium avocados, sliced

2 heaping cups chopped lettuce

Vegan mayonnaise

Ketchup, store-bought or homemade (page 265)

This classic vegan burger combo is a crowd-pleaser. They're attractive to look at, with whole black beans and vibrant yellow corn kernels peeking out. I guarantee it will be one of those burgers you make over and over again. It's like chili, but in burger form, with black beans, corn, jalapeño, lots of chili spices, and some fresh lime juice. For a less spicy option, you can skip the jalapeño.

Serves 5 (makes 5 patties)

Preheat the oven to 375°F. Line a baking sheet with parchment paper or a silicone mat. Set aside.

Heat the olive oil in a medium skillet over medium heat. Add the onion and cook for about 5 minutes, or until translucent. Add the garlic, jalapeño, oregano, smoked paprika, cumin, garlic powder, chili powder, and a generous pinch of salt. Cook for about 1 minute, or until fragrant, stirring constantly.

Transfer the beans to a large bowl. Mash about three-quarters of the beans with a fork or potato masher, leaving the remaining beans whole. Add the cooked onion mixture, corn kernels, Worcestershire, lime juice, flour, bread crumbs, black pepper, ½ teaspoon salt, and cilantro. Use your hands to incorporate all the ingredients. Adjust salt to taste.

Using a ½-cup measure for each patty and your hands, form 5 patties, each about 1-inch thick. Place the patties on the prepared baking sheet and bake for 15 minutes. Flip the patties over and bake for about 10 minutes more, or until the burgers are lightly browned.

To serve: If desired, serve the patties on toasted buns with your choice of garnishes and condiments.

Irresistible Tempeh Sliders

1 (8-ounce) package **tempeh**

Marinade

2 packed tablespoons **coarsely grated apple**

2 tablespoons **low-sodium soy sauce or tamari**

1 tablespoon **maple syrup**

1 tablespoon **toasted sesame oil**

1½ teaspoons **gochujang, or** 1 teaspoon **ketchup** mixed with ½ teaspoon **sriracha**

2 **garlic cloves**, minced

½ tablespoon grated **fresh ginger**

1 **green onion** (white and green parts), thinly sliced

2 teaspoons **neutral cooking oil** (see page 18)

Serving (Optional)

2 cups packaged **coleslaw mix** (8 ounces)

2 teaspoons **rice vinegar**

1 teaspoon **low-sodium soy sauce**

1 teaspoon **toasted sesame oil**

Salt and freshly ground black pepper to taste

Vegan mayonnaise

6 **slider buns or rolls**, toasted (see page 112)

These burgers are made with crumbled tempeh and a delicious sauce that binds the tempeh together. They are simple to make, hold together really well, and are extremely scrumptious (even to those who think they don't like tempeh).

You don't have to simmer the tempeh prior to using, but I highly recommend taking this extra step as it removes the slightly bitter flavor. It also softens the tempeh, making it easier to absorb more of the marinade.

Gochujang is a Korean red chili paste that is salty, kind of meaty, sweet, and spicy. It's a handy condiment to keep around. Just a small amount packs a lot of flavor. It's delicious in stir-fries and Asian-inspired sauces, or even drizzled over a buddha bowl. But don't sweat it if you don't have any. There's an easy-peasy substitute for this recipe.

Serves 3 (makes 6 patties)

In a medium saucepan, bring enough water to cover the tempeh by about 2 inches to a boil. Add the tempeh, reduce the heat, and simmer for 3 minutes. Drain the tempeh and pat it dry. Set aside to cool before using your hands to break the tempeh into small crumbles (see page 37).

Make the marinade: In a small bowl, mix together the apple, soy sauce, maple syrup, toasted sesame oil, gochujang, garlic, and ginger.

Transfer the marinade to a large zip-top bag along with the tempeh crumbles. Seal the bag and massage the crumbles with the marinade until they are evenly coated. Set aside for 15 minutes.

Preheat the oven to 400°F. Line a baking sheet with parchment paper or a silicone mat. Set aside.

Transfer the marinated tempeh crumbles to a medium bowl and mix in the green onion. Heat the oil in a large skillet over medium-high heat. Add the tempeh and cook for 3 minutes, stirring constantly to make sure all sides of the crumbles brown. Add ¼ cup water and cook for about 5 minutes more, or until the tempeh crumbles hold together and all of the water has been absorbed.

Recipe continues

Practically Vegan

Remove from the heat and set aside for about 5 minutes, or until cool enough to handle. Using a ¼-cup measure for each patty and your hands, shape 6 patties and place them on the prepared baking sheet.

Bake the patties for 15 minutes before flipping them over. Bake for another 10 minutes.

To serve: Meanwhile, if desired, combine the coleslaw mix, rice vinegar, soy sauce, and toasted sesame oil in a medium bowl, mixing well. Season with salt and pepper. Set aside for serving.

Once the patties are done cooking, spread some vegan mayonnaise on the buns, if using. Top with the patties and coleslaw (if using).

Artichoke Pinto Burgers

Canned and jarred artichoke hearts have a lemony taste with a briny kick, which is what makes these veggie burgers so unique. They're not your everyday bean burger, that's for sure. These are a family favorite, so much so that this recipe is going to be one of our family heirlooms!

Note that the batter will feel very sticky, but fear not. That's how it's supposed to be. They're going to come out awesome if you just follow the recipe.

Serves 4 (makes 4 patties)

1 tablespoon **flax meal** (ground flaxseeds)

1 (15-ounce) can **pinto beans**, drained and rinsed, or 1½ cups cooked pintos

1 medium **red onion**, diced (about ½ cup)

1 teaspoon **chili powder**

¾ teaspoon **paprika**

½ teaspoon **garlic powder**

½ teaspoon **ground mustard seed**

¼ teaspoon **chipotle powder**

½ cup **oat flour**

2 tablespoons **low-sodium tamari or soy sauce**

1 (8.5-ounce) can or jar quartered **artichoke hearts** (about 1 cup), roughly chopped

Salt to taste

Serving (Optional)

4 **burger buns**, toasted (see page 112)

2 medium **avocados**, sliced

1 small **red onion**, thinly sliced

Aioli (page 254)

Sriracha

In a small bowl, make a "flax egg" by mixing the flax meal with 2½ tablespoons warm water. Place in the refrigerator for 15 minutes.

Preheat the oven to 375°F. Line a baking sheet with parchment paper or a silicone mat. Set aside.

In a large bowl, mash the pinto beans using your hands or a potato masher until most of the beans are smashed, with some whole beans remaining. Add the red onion, chili powder, paprika, garlic powder, ground mustard, chipotle, oat flour, and tamari. Use your hands to thoroughly incorporate the ingredients. Add the prepared flax egg and artichoke hearts, again using your hands to mix and press everything together. Season with salt.

It is best to let the patty mixture rest at room temperature for 15 minutes before forming the patties, but if you are short on time, you can skip this step.

Using ⅔ cup of the mixture for each patty and your hands, shape 4 patties and place them on the prepared baking sheet. Bake for 15 minutes before flipping them over and baking for about 10 minutes more, or until golden brown.

To serve: If desired, serve the patties on toasted buns with your choice of garnishes and condiments.

Potato Tofu Patties

3 medium **russet potatoes**, peeled and sliced into ¼-inch-thick rounds (about 4 cups)

Salt

1 tablespoon plus 1 teaspoon **olive oil**

1 large **yellow onion**, diced (about 2 cups)

1 (14-ounce) block **extra-firm tofu**, pressed and crumbled (see page 34)

1 teaspoon **garlic powder**

1 teaspoon **finely ground black pepper**

½ teaspoon **ground mustard seed**

1 large bunch of **kale**, destemmed, leaves finely chopped (about 5 cups)

2 tablespoons **nutritional yeast**

1 cup **dried bread crumbs**

¼ cup **cornstarch or arrowroot**

¼ teaspoon **kala namak** (optional)

Dash of **sriracha** (optional)

Aioli (page 254), for dipping (optional)

This recipe uses kala namak (Indian black salt) to add an umami quality to the patties. Its palatable egg-like flavor is so good with the starchy potatoes, making these burgers one of a kind. If you don't have any, you can still make these delicious patties without it. I enjoy these patties in a toasty bun with red onion, aioli, sriracha, and avocado if you're feeling the burger vibe.

Serves 5 (makes 10 patties)

Place the potatoes in a large saucepan with enough water to cover by about 2 inches. Add 1½ teaspoons salt. Bring the water to a boil, then reduce the heat and simmer the potatoes for about 7 minutes, or until fork-tender. Be careful not to overcook the potatoes. Drain them before placing them back into the hot saucepan for 30 seconds to remove excess moisture and dry them out. Transfer the potatoes to a large bowl.

Preheat the oven to 400°F. Line a baking sheet with parchment paper or a silicone mat. Set aside.

Heat the olive oil in a large skillet over medium-high heat. Add the onion, tofu, and a generous sprinkle of salt and cook for about 5 minutes, or until the onion is translucent. Add the garlic powder, black pepper, and ground mustard and cook another 30 seconds. Mix in the kale and cook for about 2 minutes more, or until it starts to wilt. Remove the skillet from the heat.

Mash the potatoes with a potato masher or fork until mostly smooth. Add the tofu mixture to the mashed potatoes. Mix in the nutritional yeast, bread crumbs, and cornstarch and add the kala namak (if using) and salt to taste. Use your hands to incorporate the ingredients until the batter is doughlike in texture.

Using a heaping ½-cup measure for each patty and your hands, form 10 patties. Place the patties on the prepared baking sheet and bake for 15 minutes, then flip them over. Bake for about another 15 minutes, or until golden brown on both sides. Allow the patties to rest for a few minutes to firm up before serving.

If desired, add a dash of sriracha to the aioli and serve as a dipping sauce.

Chickpea Quinoa Patties

2 tablespoons **flax meal** (ground flaxseeds)

1½ cups **cooked quinoa** (about ½ cup uncooked)

½ medium **sweet potato**, peeled and grated (¾ cup)

¼ cup chopped **green onions** (white parts only)

1 **garlic clove**, minced

½ **jalapeño**, seeded and minced

⅓ cup **dried bread crumbs**

⅓ cup **garbanzo (chickpea) flour**

½ teaspoon **onion powder**

¼ teaspoon **ground cumin**

¼ teaspoon **chili powder**

¼ teaspoon **smoked paprika**

¼ teaspoon **chipotle powder**

¼ teaspoon **dried oregano**

¾ teaspoon **salt**, or to taste

1 cup **cooked chickpeas**, drained and rinsed

Aioli (page 254), for dipping (optional)

I can't help myself. Once these crispy patties come out of the oven, I immediately dig in! I love the combination of the crispy quinoa with the creamy texture of the whole chickpeas. If you manage to get ahold of some tricolor quinoa, use it. It looks fabulous!

These patties are best eaten bun-less, and paired with a side. I enjoy eating mine with a salad and some Aioli (page 254) for dipping. But you can opt to make them a bit larger (½ cup batter for each patty) and serve them as burgers on buns with your choice of toppings.

This recipe uses garbanzo flour (also called chickpea flour), which is made from dried chickpeas. It has a unique, nutty flavor that lends itself to both savory and sweet dishes. Not only does it add a delicious flavor profile to these patties, but it's also gluten-free and has a decent amount of protein.

Serves 2 (makes 6 patties)

Preheat the oven to 400°F. Line a baking sheet with parchment paper or a silicone mat. Set aside.

In a small bowl, make 2 "flax eggs" by mixing the flax meal with 5 tablespoons warm water. Set aside for at least 10 minutes.

In a large bowl, combine the cooked quinoa, sweet potato, green onion, garlic, jalapeño, bread crumbs, garbanzo flour, prepared flax eggs, onion powder, cumin, chili powder, smoked paprika, chipotle, oregano, and salt. Use your hands to thoroughly incorporate the ingredients. Fold in the chickpeas until they are evenly distributed.

Using a ⅓-cup measure for each patty and your hands, form 6 patties. Transfer them to the prepared baking sheet.

Bake for 15 minutes, then flip them over. Bake for another 10 to 15 minutes, until crispy.

Serve with aioli, if desired.

Cheesy Broccoli Fritters

⅔ cup **cooked chickpeas**, or about ½ (15-ounce) can chickpeas, drained and rinsed

2 teaspoons **olive oil** (for sautéing the chickpeas; optional)

Salt

1 medium head **broccoli**, cut into large florets

1 tablespoon **flax meal** (ground flaxseeds)

⅔ cup **garbanzo (chickpea) flour**

2 tablespoons **nutritional yeast**

¼ teaspoon **garlic powder**

¼ teaspoon **onion powder**

¼ teaspoon **paprika**

⅓ cup **unsweetened nondairy milk**

Neutral cooking oil (see page 18), for pan-frying

Aioli (page 254), for dipping (optional)

Chickpeas and broccoli are on my shortlist of favorite foods. It's kind of ridiculous that I'm calling it a shortlist when I have at least one hundred favorite foods, but that's what happens when you're passionate about plant-based foods, I guess.

I'm doubling down on chickpeas here with the use of garbanzo flour (or chickpea flour), made from dried chickpeas. I highly recommend trying out this gluten-free flour. It has a unique flavor and is also a healthy option for sweet foods like pancakes and muffins, as well as savory fritters, patties, tortillas, and crepes, and for thickening stews. Plus, it's high in protein, making these some high-protein fritters.

The buds from the broccoli florets are used here to make the fritters. The buds are the small, dark green parts at the top of the florets. Remove these with a sharp knife and add them to the batter. You can use the remaining parts of the florets in a soup or chili.

Sautéing the chickpeas before adding them to the batter is optional, but it provides a crispier texture. You can skip this step and add them to the batter, without sautéing, before you form the fritters.

Serves 2 (makes about 6 fritters)

If you prefer crispier chickpeas, place them in a medium bowl. Add the olive oil and ¼ teaspoon salt. Use your hands to rub the chickpeas until they are evenly coated in the oil. In a large nonstick skillet over medium-high heat, sauté the chickpeas for 5 minutes, stirring to crisp all sides. Transfer the chickpeas to a large plate.

Add water to a medium saucepan, about 1 inch high. Bring the water to a gentle boil. Place the broccoli florets in a steamer basket and carefully place the basket into the saucepan. Reduce the heat to medium and cover with a tightly fitting lid. Steam the broccoli florets for about 5 minutes, or until just tender. Remove the basket carefully from the saucepan and transfer the florets to a large cutting board. Using a sharp knife, slice the buds (darker green parts) from the tops of the florets. Transfer 1 cup of the buds to a small bowl. Set aside.

Recipe continues

Meanwhile, in a small bowl, mix the flax meal with 3 tablespoons warm water to make a "flax egg." Set aside for at least 10 minutes to gel.

In a medium bowl, mix together the garbanzo flour, nutritional yeast, garlic powder, onion powder, paprika, and ¾ teaspoon salt. Add the nondairy milk, flax egg, and broccoli buds and stir to combine.

Add the chickpeas and mix to incorporate all the ingredients.

Add enough neutral oil to cover the base of a large skillet to a depth of about ¼ inch. Heat the oil over medium-high heat. (To test if the oil is hot enough, drop a small amount of the batter into the skillet. It will sizzle immediately once the oil is ready.)

Use about 2 tablespoons of batter to form each fritter. Fit as many fritters into the skillet as possible without overcrowding, making sure to leave some space so they can be flipped. Cook for 2 to 3 minutes a side, until a dark golden brown. Do not flip before the underside has browned. Add more oil as needed.

Place the fritters onto paper towels to drain any excess oil. Serve with aioli for dipping, if desired.

Chickpea Fritters

¾ cup **whole-wheat pastry flour or all-purpose flour**

1 teaspoon **ground cumin**

½ teaspoon **cayenne pepper**

¼ teaspoon **paprika**

¼ teaspoon **garlic powder**

¼ teaspoon **onion powder**

½ teaspoon **salt**

2 teaspoons **maple syrup**

¾ cup diced **red bell pepper**

¼ cup diced **red onion**

¼ cup **cooked chickpeas**

2 tablespoons chopped **fresh parsley**

Neutral cooking oil (see page 18), for pan-frying

Sweet & Spicy Dipping Sauce (page 260), for dipping (optional)

These chickpea fritters make a complete dinner when served with a side salad or some veggies. They can also be a side dish.

Beware, the batter for these will feel very sticky. Don't panic. That's how fritter batters are meant to be. Just dollop the batter into the hot oil and flip after 2 to 3 minutes, or once the underside is golden brown, and they'll be perfectly crisp.

Serves 2 (makes about 10 fritters)

In a large bowl, whisk together the flour, cumin, cayenne, paprika, garlic powder, onion powder, and salt. Add ½ cup water and the maple syrup. Mix well until there are no lumps remaining.

Fold in the bell pepper, red onion, chickpeas, and parsley.

Add enough oil to cover the base of a large skillet to a depth of about ⅛ inch. Heat the oil over medium-high heat. (To test if the oil is hot enough, drop a small amount of the batter into the skillet. It will sizzle immediately once the oil is ready.)

For each fritter, add ⅛ cup batter to the skillet, using a spoon to scoop the batter out of the dry measuring cup and into the skillet, as well as to flatten the batter a little once it is in the skillet. Fit as many fritters into the skillet as possible without overcrowding, making sure to leave enough space to flip them. Cook for 2 to 3 minutes a side, until a dark golden brown. Do not flip before the underside has browned. Add more oil as needed.

Serve with dipping sauce, if desired.

Sweet Potato Falafel with Yogurt Drizzle Sauce

The biggest pitfall people run into when making falafels is that they use cooked chickpeas. Dried chickpeas are essential to getting that perfect texture that good falafels are known for. Sure, there might be an extra step of remembering to soak those bad boys overnight, but it's well worth it.

Plan ahead and soak 2 cups dried chickpeas the night before. Simply add your chickpeas to a medium bowl with enough water to cover by about 2 inches. If you forget to soak them before bed, you can do it in your sleep. It's that easy! Let them sit overnight until you're ready to drain them and make your falafels.

Serves 3 (makes about 10 falafels)

2 medium **sweet potatoes**, peeled and cut into 1-inch pieces (about 4 cups)

2 tablespoons **olive oil**, plus more for drizzling

2 cups dried **chickpeas**, soaked overnight, drained, and rinsed

3 **garlic cloves**, minced

2 tablespoons **freshly squeezed lemon juice**

½ cup **all-purpose flour or whole-wheat pastry flour**

½ cup finely chopped **red onion**

½ cup **fresh parsley** leaves, chopped

2 teaspoons **ground coriander**

2 teaspoons **ground cumin**

½ teaspoon **ground turmeric**

½ teaspoon **finely ground black pepper**

1 teaspoon **salt**, or to taste

Neutral cooking oil (see page 18), for pan-frying

Serving

3 large **pita rounds** (about 9 inches), warmed

Preheat the oven to 450°F. Line two baking sheets with parchment paper or a silicone mat.

Place the sweet potato into a medium bowl and drizzle with enough olive oil to lightly coat. Use your hands to rub the oil on the sweet potato pieces. Transfer the sweet potato to one of the prepared baking sheets and roast for 15 to 20 minutes, until fork-tender.

In a food processor, combine 2 cups of the roasted sweet potato pieces, the soaked chickpeas, garlic, lemon juice, and 2 tablespoons olive oil. Pulse until mostly smooth, with some small bits of chickpeas remaining.

Transfer the mixture to a large bowl. Add the flour, red onion, parsley, coriander, cumin, turmeric, black pepper, and salt. Mix well to fully incorporate the ingredients. Adjust salt to taste.

Scoop out about 2 tablespoons of the falafel mixture at a time. Shape it into small patties, about ½ inch thick.

Recipe continues

Practically Vegan

1 small **cucumber**, diced

2 medium **avocados**, sliced

1 small **red onion**, sliced

¼ cup **fresh parsley** leaves, chopped

Yogurt Drizzle Sauce (page 255), **Tzatziki** (page 255), or **tahini**, for drizzling

In a large nonstick skillet, heat enough neutral oil to reach halfway up the sides of each falafel, about ⅛ inch high. Pan-fry the falafels for 3 to 5 minutes on each side, until golden brown. Transfer the falafels to the other prepared baking sheet and bake for about 20 minutes, or until crispy, flipping them over after 10 minutes. (Alternatively, place the falafels onto the prepared baking sheet without frying and bake for about 25 minutes, or until golden brown on both sides, flipping them over after 15 minutes.)

To serve: If desired, heat a large frying pan or nonstick skillet over medium-high heat. Coat the pan lightly with olive oil and heat the pita rounds for about 2 minutes on each side, or until warmed through.

Cut about 1 inch off the tops of the pita rounds to reveal the pockets. Stuff each pita with about 3 falafels, some cucumber, avocado, red onion, and parsley. Drizzle with yogurt drizzle sauce, tzaziki, or tahini.

Cheesy Tofu Scramble Bagels

1 (14-ounce) block **extra-firm tofu**, pressed (see page 34)

½ cup **unsweetened nondairy milk**

1½ teaspoons **Dijon mustard**

2 tablespoons plus ½ teaspoon **nutritional yeast**

¾ teaspoon **chili powder**

½ teaspoon **ground turmeric**

½ teaspoon **garlic powder**

⅛ teaspoon **kala namak** (optional)

1 tablespoon **olive oil**

Salt and freshly ground black pepper to taste

Serving

3 **plain bagels**, halved horizontally

Vegan butter

2 medium **avocados**, sliced

Hot sauce (optional)

These tofu scramble bagels are just the thing for those days when you're craving breakfast for dinner. That happens a lot in my house!

The addition of kala namak (Indian black salt) and nutritional yeast give this dish an eggy and cheesy flavor that might trick you into believing you are eating a legit cheesy scrambled egg. Not to mention the yellow color from the turmeric.

If you don't have any kala namak, you can still make the recipe without it; you just won't get that same distinct eggy flavor.

Add a drizzle of hot sauce for an extra kick. I'm a big fan of Sky Valley Hot Sauce, and The Wizard's Hot Stuff, but almost any hot sauce will hit the spot.

Serves 3

In a large bowl, use a fork to gently mash the tofu, leaving some larger chunks.

In a medium bowl, mix the nondairy milk, mustard, nutritional yeast, chili powder, turmeric, garlic powder, and kala namak (if using). Set aside.

Heat the olive oil in a large nonstick skillet over medium heat. Cook the tofu for about 10 minutes, or until lightly browned. Use a spatula to gently turn the tofu so it cooks evenly, without breaking it apart too much.

Add the sauce to the skillet and gently mix the tofu into the sauce, keeping the tofu pieces intact.

Season with salt and pepper.

To serve: Toast the bagels. Spread each side with vegan butter. Top each half with avocado slices, tofu scramble, and a dash of hot sauce, if desired.

Tempeh Sweet Potato Hash Tortillas

1 (8-ounce) package **tempeh**

Marinade

2 tablespoons **coconut aminos**

1 tablespoon **Dijon mustard**

2 teaspoons **maple syrup**

½ teaspoon **dried oregano**

½ teaspoon **garlic powder**

½ teaspoon **smoked paprika**

¼ teaspoon **kala namak** (optional)

⅛ teaspoon **chipotle powder**

⅛ teaspoon **ancho chile powder** (optional)

2 tablespoons **olive oil**

1 large **sweet potato**, peeled and cut into ½-inch pieces (about 2½ cups)

1 small **red onion**, thinly sliced

1 medium **red bell pepper**, thinly sliced

½ teaspoon **garlic powder**

½ teaspoon **ground cumin**

½ teaspoon **chili powder**

2 tablespoons **nutritional yeast**

1½ tablespoons **low-sodium tamari or soy sauce**

These skillet sweet potatoes are cooked until golden brown and almost caramelized on the outside. I think this is my favorite way of cooking sweet potatoes. It requires a bit more babysitting, but the rest of the dish comes together super quickly.

Hash is often served with a sunny-side up egg on top, but I added kala namak to the recipe to get that eggy flavor. It's optional, but it's well worth keeping this Indian black salt in your pantry if you plan on doing a lot of vegan cooking.

Simmering the tempeh prior to use is also optional, but I highly recommend taking this extra step as it removes the slightly bitter flavor. It also softens the tempeh, making it easier for it to absorb more of the marinade.

Serves 3 (makes 6 tortillas)

In a medium saucepan, bring enough water to cover the tempeh by about 2 inches to a boil. Add the tempeh and reduce the heat. Simmer for 3 minutes. Drain the tempeh and pat dry. Set aside to cool. Use your hands to break up the tempeh into small crumbles (see page 37).

Make the marinade: In a medium bowl, combine the coconut aminos, mustard, maple syrup, oregano, garlic powder, smoked paprika, kala namak (if using), chipotle powder, and ancho chile powder (if using). Add the tempeh crumbles and use your hands to rub the crumbles with the marinade until they are evenly coated. Set aside.

Heat the olive oil in a large nonstick skillet over medium-high heat. Add the sweet potato and cook for about 7 minutes, or until the potato starts to brown, stirring frequently.

Add the tempeh and continue to cook for another 3 to 5 minutes, stirring frequently, until the sweet potato is almost fork-tender.

Add the red onion and red bell pepper. Cook for about 3 minutes more, or until the onion just starts to soften. Add the garlic powder, cumin, chili powder, and nutritional yeast and cook for 1 more minute.

1 tablespoon **freshly squeezed lime juice**

Salt and freshly ground black pepper to taste

Serving

6 soft (6-inch) **tortillas**

2 medium **avocados**, chopped

2 **limes**, cut into wedges

⅓ cup chopped **fresh cilantro**

Mix in the tamari and lime juice. Season with salt and pepper.

To serve: Stack the tortillas and wrap them in a damp paper towel. Microwave for about 15 seconds, or until warmed through (optional).

Evenly divide and place the hash down the center of the tortillas. Add avocado and a squeeze of fresh lime juice. Top with fresh cilantro. Fold the tortillas around the filling and enjoy.

Chickpea "Tuna" Salad Wraps

1 (15-ounce) can **chickpeas**, drained and rinsed, or 1½ cups cooked chickpeas

⅓ cup **vegan mayonnaise**

1½ teaspoons **sriracha**, or to taste

Zest of ½ large **lemon**

1 tablespoon plus 1 teaspoon **freshly squeezed lemon juice**

½ small **red onion**, diced small (about ⅓ cup)

2 **celery stalks**, diced (about ¼ cup)

½ teaspoon **dulse flakes or granules** (optional)

¼ teaspoon **garlic powder**

1 tablespoon chopped **fresh dill**

Salt and freshly ground black pepper to taste

Serving

3 (8-inch) **flour tortillas**, or 1 head Bibb or other butter lettuce

2 medium **tomatoes**, thinly sliced

2 small **avocados**, sliced

You won't miss the tuna in this chickpea salad. The texture is almost identical to traditional tuna salad, and the seaweed flakes (or granules) mimic the scent and taste of tuna. Seaweed flakes have the added benefit of being rich in iodine, a mineral that's often lacking in our diets. I usually buy dulse granules, because some types of seaweed, specifically kombu, can have dangerously high levels of iodine, which can be detrimental to the thyroid if consumed in large amounts.

There are many different ways to serve your chickpea "tuna" salad. You can make wraps using tortillas or lettuce leaves. Or you can use it as a filling for sandwiches or as a topping for open-faced toasts. It's also yummy when scooped up with Pita Chips (page 243). There are so many possibilities from one simple recipe! (To be honest, mine rarely makes it to the serving stage. My kids and I usually end up eating it straight from the bowl as soon as it's ready.)

Serves 3 (makes 3 wraps)

Place the chickpeas in a large bowl. Use a fork or potato masher to roughly mash about three-quarters of the chickpeas, leaving the rest whole.

Add the mayonnaise, sriracha, lemon zest and juice, red onion, celery, dulse flakes (if using), and garlic powder. Mix well to combine.

Gently fold in the dill. Season with salt and pepper.

To serve: Stack the tortillas (if using) and wrap them in a damp paper towel. Microwave for about 15 seconds, or until warmed through (optional).

Evenly divide and place the chickpea "tuna" salad down the center of the tortillas or large lettuce leaves. Add tomato and avocado. Tightly roll up each wrap, slice in half, and enjoy.

Tofu Beef Tacos

(Makes 3½ Cups Tofu Beef)

1½ cups **walnuts**

1 tablespoon **nutritional yeast**

1 teaspoon **oregano**

¾ teaspoon **smoked paprika**

¾ teaspoon **garlic powder**

¾ teaspoon **onion powder**

½ teaspoon **ground cumin**

½ teaspoon **chili powder**

¼ teaspoon **cayenne pepper**

2 tablespoons **low-sodium soy sauce or tamari**

2 tablespoons **tomato paste**

2 tablespoons **olive oil**

1 tablespoon **maple syrup**

1 (14-ounce) block **extra-firm tofu**, pressed and crumbled (see page 34)

1 small **yellow onion**, finely diced

2 large **garlic cloves**, minced

Salt and freshly ground black pepper to taste

Serving

10 soft **tortillas** (7- or 8-inch), **or** 10 hard shell **corn tacos**

Easy Guacamole (page 252) **or** 4 large **avocados**, mashed

Sour Cream (page 249)

2 heads **iceberg lettuce**, finely chopped

Tofu beef is a great way to add plant-based protein to your dinner. It's loaded with the essential plant-based omega-3 fatty acid alpha-linolenic acid (ALA) that's so good for our hearts. Walnuts are the only tree nut that are an excellent source of ALA.

This is a fabulous substitute for ground meat in any dish. Think classic lasagna, shepherd's pie, moussaka, spaghetti Bolognese, and all those other meaty dishes you may miss. Or simply serve with a grain or some slurpy noodles. I enjoy pairing mine with steamed rice and adding a side of Garlicky Kale (page 201) for a quick and nourishing dinner. I usually make a big batch of tofu beef on Sunday nights to use in different recipes throughout the week.

For this recipe, we are using it as a filling for tacos. If you are short on time or just don't feel like working too hard, sub the guacamole with mashed avocados. The "beef" is so delicious, no one will notice!

Soft tortillas or hard shell tacos can be used for serving the tofu beef. If you choose hard shell tacos, preheat the oven to 375°F before you start making the tofu beef. This way you won't have to wait long to devour your warm and crispy tacos.

Serves 5 (makes 10 tacos)

Preheat the oven to 375°F if using hard shell tacos.

In a food processor, pulse the walnuts enough times for large crumbles to form. (Be careful not to overdo it. You do not want the walnuts to become flour.) Set aside.

In a large bowl, mix together the nutritional yeast, oregano, smoked paprika, garlic powder, onion powder, cumin, chili powder, cayenne, soy sauce, tomato paste, 1 tablespoon of the olive oil, and the maple syrup. Add the tofu crumbles and chopped walnuts. Use your hands to rub the spice mixture on the tofu and walnut crumbles until they are evenly coated.

Heat the remaining 1 tablespoon olive oil in a large nonstick skillet over medium-high heat. Add the onion and cook for about 3 minutes, or until translucent. Add the garlic and cook for 30 seconds more. Add the tofu-walnut mixture plus 1 tablespoon water. Cook for 5 to 7 minutes, until the mixture just becomes dry, stirring frequently. Remove from the heat. Season with salt and pepper.

To serve: For soft tacos, stack the tortillas and wrap them in a damp paper towel. Microwave for about 15 seconds, or until warmed through (optional).

For hard-shell tacos, place the taco shells onto a baking sheet and bake for about 5 minutes, or until crispy.

If using soft tortillas, fold each one into a U shape. Fill each soft or hard taco shell with about ⅓ cup tofu beef, ¼ cup guacamole (or mashed avocado), a dollop of sour cream, and chopped lettuce.

Chapter 5

Asian Fake-Out

I don't know about you, but I love Asian-inspired take-out. In my opinion, it's one of the few cuisines that tastes even better the next day! Why do I call this chapter "fake-out"? Because these recipes mimic my favorite take-out dishes but with all plant-based ingredients and a lot less salt.

There are many elements to Asian cuisine, but here I'm giving you lots of dinner stir-fry recipes, so make sure you brush up on those Stir-Fry Basics (page 37) to remind yourself of the dos and don'ts for the perfect stir-fry.

Swaps & Substitutions

These sauces below are all interchangeable. When a recipe in this chapter calls for one of these sauces, feel free to substitute it with a different sauce on this list. The quantities are close enough that these swaps can be made seamlessly. (See chapter 8 for complete sauce recipes.)

- Basic Stir-Fry Sauce
- Hoisin Stir-Fry Sauce
- Sesame Stir-Fry Sauce
- Sweet & Spicy Gingery Stir-Fry Sauce
- Teriyaki Sauce

Tofu Veggie Fried Rice

2 cups cooked jasmine rice, preferably refrigerated for at least 8 hours, or ¾ cup uncooked jasmine rice

Tofu

2 tablespoons low-sodium tamari or soy sauce

2 teaspoons rice vinegar

½ teaspoon toasted sesame oil

½ teaspoon ground white pepper

1 (14-ounce) block extra-firm tofu, pressed and cut into ½-inch cubes (see page 34)

Stir-Fry

2 tablespoons neutral cooking oil (see page 18), plus more as needed

2 tablespoons minced fresh ginger

½ teaspoon crushed red pepper (optional)

1 cup diced carrots

1 cup frozen green peas

1 cup frozen corn kernels

½ cup thinly sliced green onions (white and green parts, about 6 green onions)

2 tablespoons low-sodium tamari or soy sauce

2 teaspoons sesame oil

⅛ teaspoon ground white pepper

½ cup roasted peanuts (optional)

Salt to taste

Fried rice is so much better when made from leftover rice. While you can use freshly cooked rice in this recipe if you have no leftovers, it will have a slightly mushier texture, but it will still be yummy.

A practical thing about this recipe is you can use frozen veggies without defrosting them first—a huge time-saver.

Plan ahead: You will need 2 cups cooked rice prepared the night before and refrigerated.

Serves 4

Remove the cooked rice from the refrigerator and set aside. If you are not using leftover rice, cook the ¾ cup rice according to the package directions, then set aside to cool.

Prepare the tofu: In a medium baking dish, mix together the tamari, rice vinegar, toasted sesame oil, and white pepper. Add the tofu. Use your hands to gently toss the tofu in the marinade until all the pieces are well coated. Set aside for 15 minutes.

Make the stir-fry: Heat 1 tablespoon of the oil in a large nonstick skillet or wok over medium-high heat until shimmering. Add the tofu and cook for about 7 minutes, or until golden brown on all sides. Move the cubes around every 1 to 2 minutes for even browning. Remove the skillet from the heat. Transfer the tofu to a baking sheet or plate.

Wipe the skillet clean with a paper towel and return it to the stove. Heat 1 tablespoon of the oil over medium-high heat. Cook the ginger and crushed red pepper (if using) for about 10 seconds, or until fragrant, stirring constantly. Add the carrots and cook for 1 minute more. Add the peas and corn and cook for about 30 seconds, or until just heated through.

Drizzle more oil into the skillet if needed. Add the rice and green onions and sauté for 2 minutes, breaking up the rice with a spatula while mixing it with the vegetables.

Drizzle the tamari and sesame oil around the edge of the skillet. Sprinkle the white pepper on top of the rice. Continue to cook, while mixing in the seasonings, for about 20 seconds, or until all the seasonings are incorporated and the rice is warmed through.

Reduce the heat to medium-low and add the tofu and peanuts (if using). Stir to combine. Add salt to taste.

Tempeh Bacon Fried Rice

3 cups cooked jasmine rice, preferably refrigerated for at least 8 hours, or 1 cup uncooked jasmine rice

Tempeh Bacon (page 221)

1 tablespoon neutral cooking oil (see page 18)

2 medium carrots, diced small (about 1 cup)

1 cup frozen green peas, thawed and drained

1 tablespoon grated fresh ginger

4 garlic cloves, minced

½ cup thinly sliced green onions (white and green parts, about 6 green onions)

3 tablespoons low-sodium soy sauce or tamari

2 teaspoons toasted sesame oil

Salt to taste

I actually came up with the idea for this recipe in a dream. Yes, I dream about food on a regular basis. Doesn't everyone? With the delicious addition of Tempeh Bacon here, you won't miss the egg, or meat, in this fried rice. I'm certain—after all, it's called "tempeh bacon" for a reason! The tempeh *actually* tastes like bacon. Now, I haven't had bacon in decades, but I did get confirmation from my friends who have. So don't avoid this dish because you think you don't like tempeh; it's bacon, remember! And if you have kids, this was a winner dish with mine. "Is there more, Mummy?"

Plan ahead: For best results, cook your rice the night before and store it in the refrigerator. You will also need the full recipe for Tempeh Bacon (page 221). This is the only part that requires any real work here, but it's so worth it. Otherwise, the recipe comes together super quickly.

Serves 2 to 3

Remove the rice from the refrigerator and set aside. If you are not using leftover rice, cook 1 cup rice according to the package directions, then set aside to cool.

Cut the tempeh bacon into ½-inch squares. Set aside.

Heat the neutral oil in a large nonstick skillet or wok over medium-high heat. Add the carrots and peas and cook for about 3 minutes, or until the carrots just start to become tender but not softened.

Add the ginger and garlic and cook for about 1 minute, or until fragrant.

Add the tempeh bacon squares and cook for about 1 minute more, or until just warmed through.

Add the green onions and cook for another 30 seconds.

Add the soy sauce and stir. Add the rice and mix to combine. Cook for about 3 minutes, or until the rice is warmed through, stirring frequently so it heats evenly.

Remove the skillet from the heat and mix in the toasted sesame oil. Season with salt.

Sesame Noodle Veggie Stir-Fry

8 ounces **udon, lo mein, or rice noodles**

1 teaspoon **toasted sesame oil**

1 (14-ounce) block **firm or extra-firm tofu**, pressed and cut into ¾-inch cubes (see page 34)

1 tablespoon **cornstarch or arrowroot**

¼ teaspoon **ground white pepper**

¼ teaspoon **salt**

1 tablespoon plus 1 teaspoon **neutral cooking oil** (see page 18)

1 head **broccoli**, cut into bite-size florets (about 3 cups)

1 medium **red bell pepper**, thinly sliced (about 2 cups)

1 large **carrot**, cut into matchsticks (about 1 cup)

1 tablespoon minced **fresh ginger**

4 large **garlic cloves**, minced

Hoisin Stir-Fry Sauce (page 261)

1 tablespoon **toasted sesame seeds** (see page 40), for garnish

3 **green onions**, sliced (green parts only), for garnish

I've got your back, friends. I told you I'm all about versatility. The veggies in this recipe can easily be substituted. Sugar snap peas, baby corn, green beans, and snow peas are all good substitutes. Simply follow the quantities in the recipe. Cut your veggies into bite-size pieces when necessary and cook the firmer ones first.

The recipe uses hoisin sauce, which can be a little pricey at the store. I've tried to make my own, but I was challenged to make one quite as delicious as the store-bought ones. It adds a unique flavor that really elevates the dish. I highly recommend investing in a bottle. You won't regret it.

And about that "toasted" sesame oil—not to be confused with the lighter sesame oil. It is a finishing oil that has a strong sesame flavor and should be added at the end of the cooking process to flavor the dish. The rich sesame flavor comes from toasting the sesame seeds. If you don't have toasted sesame oil, you can use standard sesame oil. It will still be delicious, but the flavor won't be quite as intense.

This easy dish will be all gone before you can say "toasted sesame oil"!

Serves 3 to 4

Cook the noodles according to the package directions. Drain and transfer to a medium bowl. Toss with the toasted sesame oil and set aside.

Place the tofu into a large plastic zip-top bag or reusable container with the cornstarch, white pepper, and salt. Gently move the tofu around in the bag until all the cubes are evenly coated. Set aside.

Heat a large nonstick skillet over medium-high heat. Add 1 tablespoon of the neutral oil to the hot skillet and swirl it around until the oil coats the bottom. Once the oil is hot, add the tofu and cook, undisturbed, for 3 to 4 minutes, until it is golden brown on the bottom. Flip the tofu cubes and continue cooking for about 3 minutes more, or until all sides are golden brown. Transfer the tofu to a large baking sheet or dish.

Add the broccoli to the hot skillet along with 1 tablespoon water. Cover with a tight-fitting lid. Allow the broccoli to steam for about 1 minute, or until slightly tender. Remove the lid and add the bell pepper and carrots. Cook for 1 to

2 minutes, until tender-crisp, alternating between stirring and letting the vegetables sit to brown.

Move the vegetables to the outer edges of the skillet. Add the remaining 1 teaspoon neutral oil to the center of the skillet. Once the oil is hot, add the ginger and garlic to the center and cook for 30 seconds, stirring constantly so the garlic does not burn.

Add the tofu and hoisin stir-fry sauce. Mix the vegetables, tofu, and sauce together and cook for about 3 minutes, or until the sauce starts to thicken. Using a pair of tongs, mix in the noodles and cook for about 1 more minute, or until just warmed through. Garnish with toasted sesame seeds and green onions and serve immediately.

Sweet & Spicy Cauliflower Wings

Nowadays you can find cauliflower turned into all sorts of things. Here, we're going to turn cauliflower into wings, encased in a delicious crispy batter that's really quite divine and coated with a delectable sweet-and-spicy sauce. These are best served immediately. If you leave them hanging out for too long, they'll lose the crispiness that makes them so tantalizing.

Serve your "wings" with a simple side of steamed rice or a different grain of your choice. Additional serving suggestions are listed below.

Serves 2 to 3

¾ cup **all-purpose flour**

2 teaspoons **garlic powder**

½ teaspoon **ground white pepper**

½ teaspoon **salt**

¾ cups **unsweetened nondairy milk**

1 medium **cauliflower**, stemmed and cut into bite-size florets (about 3 cups)

Sauce

¼ cup **low-sodium soy sauce or tamari**

2 tablespoons **rice vinegar**

1 tablespoon **sriracha**

1½ teaspoons **toasted sesame oil**

1½ to 2 tablespoons **maple syrup**, or to taste

1 tablespoon **cornstarch**

2 teaspoons **sesame oil**

2 **garlic cloves**, minced

1 teaspoon minced **fresh ginger**

2 teaspoons **toasted sesame seeds** (see page 40), for garnish

Preheat the oven to 450°F. Line a baking sheet with parchment paper or a silicone mat. Set aside.

In a large bowl, whisk together the flour, garlic powder, white pepper, and salt. Stir in the nondairy milk and mix well until a smooth batter forms. Stir in the cauliflower until all the florets are coated with the batter. Place them on the prepared baking sheet, first shaking each one to remove excess batter.

Roast for about 20 minutes, or until golden brown. Then turn on the broiler and broil for 2 to 3 minutes more, until crispy.

Meanwhile, make the sauce: In a medium bowl, mix together the soy sauce, rice vinegar, sriracha, toasted sesame oil, and ¼ cup water. Stir in 1½ tablespoons maple syrup, then adjust to taste. Whisk in the cornstarch until fully dissolved.

Once the cauliflower is done roasting, heat the sesame oil in a large nonstick skillet over medium heat. Add the garlic and ginger and cook for about 30 seconds, or until fragrant, stirring constantly. Add the sauce and cook for 1 to 2 minutes more, until the sauce starts to thicken. Stir in the cauliflower and cook for about 1 minute, until just warmed through. Garnish with toasted sesame seeds and serve.

Other Serving Suggestions

Asian-Inspired Crunchy Salad with Sesame Ginger Dressing (page 196)
Garlicky Rice (page 235)
Coconut Quinoa (page 235)
Spicy Peanut Miso Noodles (page 238)
Sesame Garlic Ramen Noodles (page 240)

Practically Vegan

Chickpea Bell Pepper Stir-Fry

1 tablespoon **sesame oil**

2 teaspoons minced **fresh ginger**

2 (15-ounce) cans **chickpeas**, drained and rinsed, or 3 cups cooked chickpeas

2 medium **red bell peppers**, cut into ½-inch pieces

Basic Stir-Fry Sauce (page 261)

Dark soy sauce is used to flavor this dish, and to give it a rich brown color as the sauce caramelizes. It's thicker, darker, and slightly sweeter than regular soy sauce, and can be used in sauces, fried rice, and noodles to darken their color. Its downside, however, is that it's quite a bit higher in sodium than regular soy sauce, so it should be used more sparingly. In the grand scheme of things, this dish is still way less salty than any take-out meal you might order. Don't be deterred if you don't have any dark soy sauce on hand; regular soy sauce works well, too.

This recipe is very versatile. You can swap the chickpeas for Crispy Baked Tofu Cubes (page 213), if you prefer. Just add the tofu to the skillet when you add the sauce.

The bell peppers can be subbed with a different veggie. Blanched broccoli, zucchini, or summer squash would all be good in this dish. (My middle daughter hates cooked peppers, so I usually make her portion with broccoli. It's the one exception where I will short-order cook!)

Serve this with a simple side of steamed rice or a different grain of your choice. Additional serving suggestions are listed below.

Serves 6

Heat the sesame oil in a large nonstick skillet or wok over medium-high heat. Add the ginger, chickpeas, and bell pepper and sauté for 5 to 7 minutes, until the bell pepper starts to char and soften. Add the sauce and continue to stir. Cook for 4 to 5 minutes, until the sauce has thickened and starts to caramelize.

Other Serving Suggestions

Garlicky Rice (page 235)
Coconut Quinoa (page 235)
Lemony Cauliflower Rice (page 237)
Sesame Garlic Ramen Noodles (page 240)

Miso Eggplant Steaks with Spicy Peanut Noodles

Vegans have a habit of stealing carnivore terminology and applying it to their non-carnivore creations. Cauliflower has been subjected to this over and over again, and now we're doing it to eggplant with these eggplant steaks!

It's the texture and umami flavor that make these cuts of eggplant so steak-like. The miso adds an umami quality to the naturally meaty texture of the roasted eggplant, turning it into one of those "you won't miss the meat" kind of dinners.

Brushing the glaze onto the eggplant during the cooking process makes the flesh even more tender and flavorful, and the best part is that the leftover glaze becomes the sauce for the noodles. Eggplants are rich in anthocyanins, which is what gives them their unusual color. This pigment has antioxidant properties that protect your cells from damage.

Serves 2

Glaze

1½ tablespoons **dark soy sauce** or **soy sauce**

1 tablespoon **low-sodium tamari** or **soy sauce**

1½ tablespoons **maple syrup**

1 tablespoon **mellow (white) miso**

1 tablespoon smooth **peanut, almond, or cashew butter**

1 teaspoon **sesame oil**

½ teaspoon **chili-garlic sauce**

1 medium **eggplant** (about ¾ pound), sliced in half lengthwise

Sesame oil, for brushing

3 ounces **udon or rice noodles**

2 teaspoons **toasted sesame seeds**, (see page 40), for garnish

Preheat the oven to 400°F. Line a baking sheet with parchment paper or a silicone mat. Set aside.

Make the glaze: In a medium bowl, mix together the dark soy sauce, tamari, maple syrup, miso, peanut butter, sesame oil, chili-garlic sauce, and 1 tablespoon water. Make sure the miso is fully dissolved.

Score the cut sides of both eggplant halves using the tip of a small knife. Make small incisions in a crosshatch pattern on both pieces, going as deep as possible without piercing the skin. Brush the flesh side of both halves with sesame oil.

Heat a medium nonstick skillet over medium-high heat. Cook the eggplant, flesh side down, for 3 minutes. Turn over both pieces and cook the skin side for 2 minutes more. Transfer the eggplant to the prepared baking sheet, flesh side up.

Use a teaspoon to drizzle a generous amount of the glaze along the top and between the incisions in the flesh on both eggplant halves, making sure the glaze gets into all the cuts. Brush the glaze into the flesh using a pastry brush. The flesh should be fully coated with the glaze, with a thin layer on top.

Roast the eggplant steaks, flesh side up, for 10 minutes. Remove them from the oven and use the pastry brush to glaze the flesh again, basting each half until fully coated. Roast for another 7 to 10 minutes, until the desired texture is reached. Turn on the oven broiler. Brush the flesh once more with the glaze and broil for 1 minute.

Meanwhile, cook the noodles according to the package directions. Set aside.

Heat the remaining glaze in a small skillet over low heat until it is warmed through and just starts to thicken. Remove the skillet from the heat and stir in the noodles until they are fully coated in the glaze.

Garnish the eggplant and noodles with toasted sesame seeds and serve immediately.

Sticky Sesame Tofu

This is a four-ingredient sauce that turns humble tofu into a delicious protein-rich main. No chopping required, except for one garlic clove. I think we can manage that!

It's best to use 100 percent fruit jam for this recipe—the thick kind with no added sugar.

Serve your tofu with a simple side of steamed rice or a different grain of your choice. Additional serving suggestions are listed below.

Serves 3

Sticky Sauce

1 large **garlic clove**, minced

2 tablespoons **low-sodium soy sauce or tamari**

¼ cup **all-fruit apricot, orange, or peach jam**

1 teaspoon **hot sauce** (optional)

1 (14-ounce) block **extra-firm tofu**, pressed and cut into 1-inch cubes (see page 34)

1 tablespoon **cornstarch**

½ teaspoon **garlic powder**

¼ teaspoon **ground white pepper**

¼ teaspoon **salt**

1 tablespoon **sesame oil**

2 teaspoons **toasted sesame seeds** (see page 40), for garnish

Make the sticky sauce: In a small bowl, mix together the garlic, soy sauce, jam, and hot sauce (if using). Set aside.

Place the tofu into a large plastic zip-top bag or airtight container. In a small bowl, combine the cornstarch, garlic powder, white pepper, and salt and mix well. Transfer the cornstarch mixture to the zip-top bag and gently rotate the bag, moving the tofu around until all the pieces are coated.

Heat the sesame oil in a large skillet over medium-high heat. Add the tofu and sauté for 5 to 7 minutes, until golden brown on all sides. Mix in the sauce, stir, and cook for 2 to 3 minutes more, until the sauce starts to thicken and is warmed through. Sprinkle with toasted sesame seeds.

Serve immediately.

Other Serving Suggestions

Asian-Inspired Crunchy Salad with Sesame Ginger Dressing (page 196)
Garlicky Kale (page 201)
Sautéed Asparagus with Garlic "Facon" (page 202)
Maple Soy Green Beans (page 208)
Garlicky Rice (page 235)
Lemony Cauliflower Rice (page 237)
Sesame Garlic Ramen Noodles (page 240)

Tofu Lettuce Wraps

1 cup **uncooked sushi rice or other short-grain rice** (optional)

Sauce

3 tablespoons **low-sodium soy sauce or coconut aminos**

3 tablespoons **rice vinegar**

1½ teaspoons **toasted sesame oil**

5 tablespoons **hoisin sauce**

1 teaspoon **cornstarch**

1 (14-ounce) block **extra-firm tofu**, pressed and crumbled (see page 34)

Salt and ground white pepper

2 tablespoons **neutral cooking oil** (see page 18)

Cornstarch, for sprinkling

1 (8-ounce) package **baby bella (cremini) or white button mushrooms**, finely chopped

½ cup finely diced **carrots**

1 (8-ounce) can **water chestnuts**, drained and finely chopped (optional)

3 **garlic cloves**, minced

1 tablespoon minced **fresh ginger**

½ cup thinly sliced **green onions** (white and green parts, about 6 green onions)

2 tablespoons **hoisin sauce**, or to taste

Serving

2 small heads **Bibb, iceberg, or butter lettuce**

These Asian-style wraps hit the spot when you're in the mood for a light and appetizing dinner. Lettuce leaves are an easy and healthy alternative to flour-based wraps. Bibb, iceberg, and butter lettuces work best for this, and they can be used to wrap almost anything your creativity inspires.

The water chestnuts add a delicious crunch to this dish. They are usually sold canned and are available at most major supermarkets. If you can't get your hands on some, go ahead and make the recipe without them.

You may decide not to make wraps at all. This hoisin-flavored tofu mince pairs deliciously with most grains. I enjoy eating mine with a side of Garlicky Rice (page 235).

Serves 2 to 3 without rice, 4 to 5 with rice

Cook the rice (if using) according to the package directions. Set aside.

Make the sauce: In a medium bowl, mix the soy sauce, rice vinegar, toasted sesame oil, and hoisin sauce. Add the cornstarch, whisking well until no lumps remain. Set aside.

Season the crumbled tofu with a dash of salt and white pepper. In a large nonstick skillet, heat 2 teaspoons of the neutral oil over medium heat until shimmering. Add half of the crumbled tofu. Sprinkle with a generous pinch of cornstarch. Sauté until golden brown. Transfer to a large dish. Add another 1 to 2 teaspoons of the neutral oil and repeat for the remaining tofu. Set aside.

Add 2 teaspoons of the oil to the same skillet. Add the mushrooms and carrots and cook for about 4 minutes, or until the mushrooms have released their moisture. Stir in the water chestnuts (if using), garlic, and ginger. Cook for about 30 seconds, or until fragrant.

Return the tofu crumbles to the skillet and add half of the green onions. Add the sauce and cook for about 60 seconds, or until the sauce is warmed through. Add the hoisin sauce. Garnish with the remaining green onions.

To serve: Place 1 to 2 tablespoons of rice (if using) along the center of each lettuce leaf. Add a generous spoonful of the tofu mixture.

Teriyaki Pulled Jackfruit Sandwich

1 tablespoon **neutral cooking oil** (see page 18)

½ medium **yellow onion**, thinly sliced

3 **garlic cloves**, minced

1¼ teaspoons **paprika**

¼ cup **vegetable broth**

Teriyaki Sauce (page 264)

1 (14-ounce) can **young jackfruit** packed in water and sea salt, drained and rinsed

½ teaspoon **toasted sesame oil**

Serving

4 **hamburger buns**

Cabbage Slaw (page 191; optional)

Jackfruit is a tropical fruit that can be used in savory dishes before it ripens and turns sweet. In this stage of the ripening process, the jackfruit is referred to as young or green. Young jackfruit is almost flavorless and is often cooked as a vegetable, whereas ripe jackfruit is sweet and eaten raw.

Young jackfruit has a meaty texture, making it a popular plant-based meat substitute. The texture is similar to pulled pork once it's cooked in sauce; it becomes stringy and pulls apart in a similar manner.

Be sure to buy young, or green, jackfruit packed in water and sea salt. It can usually be found in the canned section of your grocery store or in Asian markets. I like to use the Native Forest brand.

I won't judge you for using store-bought teriyaki sauce instead of making your own. You're already doing a marvelous job getting a homemade dinner on the table. Take whatever shortcuts you need.

Serves 4 (makes 4 sandwiches)

Heat the neutral oil in a medium skillet over medium heat. Add the onion and cook for about 5 minutes, or until the onion is translucent. Add the garlic and paprika and cook for about another 30 seconds, or until fragrant.

Add the vegetable broth, ½ cup of the teriyaki sauce, and the jackfruit. Reduce the heat to a simmer, cover, and cook for 10 to 12 minutes, until the jackfruit can easily be shredded with a fork. Add more teriyaki sauce to taste and continue to cook uncovered, until the sauce starts to thicken and is warmed through. Remove from the heat and stir in the toasted sesame oil. (Store any remaining sauce in the refrigerator in an airtight container for up to 5 days.)

Meanwhile, preheat the oven to 350°F. Toast the buns for about 5 minutes, or until they are warmed through and lightly crispy. (Alternatively, you can toast the buns in a toaster oven.) Remove the buns and place them into a basket or bowl with a tea towel on top, or wrap them in foil, to keep them from becoming hard and crunchy.

Evenly divide the jackfruit and sauce among the burger buns. Top with the cabbage slaw, if using, and serve.

Ginger Sesame Soy Curls

8 ounces **soy curls**

1½ tablespoons **cornstarch**

1½ teaspoons **salt**

Sauce

3 tablespoons **coconut aminos**

1 tablespoon **dark soy sauce or soy sauce**

2 tablespoons **low-sodium tamari or soy sauce**

3 tablespoons **maple syrup**

2 tablespoons **rice vinegar**

2 tablespoons **toasted sesame oil**

2 teaspoons **sriracha**

1 tablespoon **cornstarch**

1½ tablespoons **sesame oil**

5 **garlic cloves**, minced

2 teaspoons minced **fresh ginger**

Low-sodium tamari or soy sauce to taste

1½ tablespoons **toasted sesame seeds** (see page 40), for garnish

Soy curls are high in protein and have a texture very similar to chicken. They're tasteless on their own but easily absorb the flavors of sauces and marinades. They're my kids' favorite meat substitute.

Soy curls can be found in some health food stores and Asian markets. While they're still not widely available at mainstream supermarkets, you're pretty much guaranteed to find them on Amazon. The brand I buy is Butler, and it's non-GMO, grown without chemical pesticides, and free from additives or preservatives.

This recipe calls for dark soy sauce. It's thicker and darker than regular soy sauce, making the dish look truer to takeout. It's a versatile ingredient, and I use it quite often. It's useful to keep it as a substitute for a portion of the soy sauce or tamari in Asian-style recipes, but it's not a pantry essential. Regular soy sauce or tamari are good substitutes.

Serve your Ginger Sesame Soy Curls with a simple side of steamed rice or a different grain of your choice. Additional serving suggestions are listed on page 160.

Serves 5

Soak the soy curls in a large bowl with enough warm water to cover by about 1½ inches for 10 minutes. (Do not soak for longer than 10 minutes or they will lose their texture.) Pour them into a colander to drain and then place them back in the bowl. Sprinkle the soy curls with the cornstarch and salt. Use your hands to gently toss them until they are evenly coated with the cornstarch.

Meanwhile, make the sauce: In a medium bowl, mix the coconut aminos, dark soy sauce, tamari, maple syrup, rice vinegar, toasted sesame oil, sriracha, and 1 tablespoon water, stirring until blended. Set aside. Make the cornstarch slurry in a small bowl by dissolving the cornstarch in 2 tablespoons water.

Heat the sesame oil in a large nonstick skillet or wok over medium-high heat. Add the garlic and ginger and cook for 30 seconds. Add the soy curls and sauté for 8 to 10 minutes, until they are golden brown and have a slightly crispy outer layer. (You may have to sauté the soy curls in batches. If the skillet is overcrowded, they will steam and not brown.)

Recipe continues

Reduce the heat to medium-low. Add the sauce and cornstarch slurry and heat, stirring constantly for 3 to 4 minutes, until warmed through. Add tamari to taste.

Garnish with toasted sesame seeds and serve.

Other Starchy Serving Suggestions

Garlicky Rice (page 235)
Coconut Quinoa (page 235)
Lemony Cauliflower Rice (page 237)
Spicy Peanut Miso Noodles (page 238)
Sesame Garlic Ramen Noodles (page 240)

Other Veggie Side Serving Suggestions

Roasted Broccoli or Cauliflower Bites (page 197)
Garlicky Kale (page 201)
Sautéed Asparagus with Garlic "Facon" (page 202)
Maple Soy Green Beans (page 208)

Chickpea Eggplant Stir-Fry in Peanut Sauce

1 medium **eggplant**, sliced into ¾-inch-thick rounds, then cut into ¾-inch pieces (about 4 cups)

Salt

1 (15-ounce) can **chickpeas**, drained and rinsed, or 1½ cups cooked chickpeas

2½ teaspoons **neutral cooking oil** (see page 18)

1 teaspoon minced **fresh ginger**

1 large **garlic clove**, minced

Peanut Sauce (page 262)

This recipe is super versatile. The peanut sauce is fabulous and pairs well with tofu, tempeh, or veggies. Get creative and give this sauce a try with other plant-based proteins and an assortment of veggies. You can substitute any nut butter you have on hand for the peanut butter. Make an almond sauce or cashew sauce. Just remember to change the name of the dish accordingly!

If you happen to be making this for dinner tonight, I'm extremely jealous. It's a favorite in my house.

Serve your stir-fry with a simple side of steamed rice, noodles, or a different grain of your choice. Additional serving suggestions are listed below.

Serves 3

Transfer the chopped eggplant to a large bowl and add a generous dash of salt. Massage the eggplant until the flesh is evenly coated with the salt. Set aside.

Rub the chickpeas between two large paper towels, or a folded kitchen towel, to remove any excess moisture.

Heat 1 teaspoon of the neutral oil in a large nonstick skillet over medium-high heat. Add the chickpeas and sauté for 3 to 4 minutes, until golden brown. Reduce the heat to medium and add the remaining 1½ teaspoons oil. Add the eggplant and cook, stirring frequently, for about 5 minutes, or until almost tender.

Add the ginger and garlic to the skillet and cook for about 1 minute more, or until fragrant. Reduce the heat to low and add the peanut sauce plus 1 tablespoon water. Gently mix in the sauce and cook for about 2 minutes more, or until warmed through. Add salt to taste.

Other Serving Suggestions

Garlicky Rice (page 235)
Coconut Quinoa (page 235)
Sesame Garlic Ramen Noodles (page 240)

Chapter 6

Comfort Food

Comfort food consists of food that typically provides nostalgic or sentimental value to someone. It is usually associated with the security of childhood. Comforting meals tend to be high in calories and carbohydrates, and not at all healthy.

My comfort foods are healthful without compromising the nurturing nature of these foods. These dishes are reminiscent of my boarding school years and the abundance of stews, creamy sauces, decadent potatoes, and cuts of meat that made up our dinners.

Tofu & Sweet Peas in Béchamel Sauce

Béchamel Sauce

1 cup **raw cashews**, soaked, drained, and rinsed (see page 39)

⅓ cup **nutritional yeast**

1 tablespoon **garlic powder**

1 teaspoon **salt**, or to taste

½ teaspoon **onion powder**

⅛ teaspoon **ground nutmeg**

⅛ teaspoon **finely ground black pepper**

1 tablespoon **olive oil**

1 (14-ounce) block **extra-firm tofu**, pressed and cut into triangles (see page 34)

½ cup **frozen green peas**, thawed and drained

This delicious béchamel sauce is full of possibilities. It pairs well with beans, lentils, pasta, and steamed or roasted veggies.

The creaminess of the sauce comes from the cashews. Although cashews sometimes get a bad rap for being overused in vegan recipes, let's not forget that they are rich in fiber and heart-healthy fats, as well as a source of plant protein, all combined to make this a very nutritious sauce, much more so than typical non-vegan creamy sauces with all that heavy cream and butter.

Serve your creamy tofu and sweet peas with a simple side of steamed rice or a different grain of your choice. Additional serving suggestions are listed below.

Serves 4

Make the béchamel sauce: Blend the cashews, nutritional yeast, garlic powder, salt, onion powder, nutmeg, black pepper, and 1½ cups water in a high-speed blender on high until smooth. Set aside.

Heat the olive oil in a large nonstick skillet over medium-high heat. Sauté the tofu for about 3 minutes on each side, or until golden brown. Transfer the tofu to a large plate and set aside.

Heat the béchamel sauce in a large saucepan over medium heat for about 5 minutes, or until it starts to thicken. Stir in the green peas and tofu and cook for about 2 minutes more, or just until heated through.

Other Serving Suggestions

Perfectly Crisp Roasted Baby Potatoes (page 224)
Smashed Potatoes (page 227)
Crispy Top Potato Rounds (page 229)
Garlicky Rice (page 235)
Coconut Quinoa (page 235)
Lemony Cauliflower Rice (page 237)

Crispy Cauliflower Steaks with Pimiento Sauce

1 cup **unsweetened nondairy milk**

1 teaspoon **apple cider vinegar**

¾ cup **all-purpose flour or oat flour**

½ cup **cornstarch**

¾ teaspoon **paprika**

½ teaspoon **garlic powder**

½ teaspoon **onion powder**

1 teaspoon **salt**

1 teaspoon **finely ground black pepper**

2½ cups **panko bread crumbs**

1 large head **cauliflower**, outer leaves removed

Neutral cooking oil (see page 18), for pan-frying

Olive oil, for drizzling

Here we go again, giving this cruciferous vegetable another identity!

Why do we call this particular cut of cauliflower a "steak"? I can't say I know for sure, but the way the cauliflower is cut lengthwise down the middle, it almost has the shape of a classic veal chop, with the harder central core mimicking the bone. You'll likely have more success if you cut your steaks on the thicker side. Thicker steaks hold together much better than thinner ones, plus they have a "meatier" texture.

The combination of these steaks with the uniquely flavored pimiento sauce is out-of-this-world delicious. Adding canned pimientos to the sauce is a game changer. They can be found in most supermarkets and provide a huge burst of flavor, especially for such a small can. Almonds are also used to make the sauce, making it rich in heart-healthy fats.

Try this sauce with roasted veggies, raw veggies, pasta, and crispy roasted potatoes. It has numerous uses beyond this recipe. I'm sure there are many more scrumptious combos I haven't yet discovered.

I like adding Chickpea Croutons (page 222) to this dish for additional protein, and a side salad for a more substantial meal. Additional serving suggestions are listed on page 168.

Serves 3 to 4

Place the almonds for the pimiento sauce in a medium bowl with enough hot water to cover by about 2 inches. Set aside.

Preheat the oven to 425°F. Line a baking sheet with parchment paper or a silicone mat. Set aside.

In a medium bowl, make vegan buttermilk by mixing together the nondairy milk and cider vinegar. Set aside.

In a large bowl, whisk the flour, cornstarch, paprika, garlic powder, onion powder, salt, and the finely ground black pepper until combined. Set aside.

Transfer the panko to a rimmed serving dish or baking sheet. Set aside.

Recipe continues

Pimiento Sauce

1 cup raw almonds

1 (7-ounce) jar whole red pimientos, drained

1 large garlic clove

¼ cup freshly squeezed lemon juice

2 teaspoons Dijon mustard

1 teaspoon sriracha

1½ teaspoons onion powder

½ teaspoon smoked paprika

¼ cup nutritional yeast

Salt and freshly ground black pepper to taste

Other Serving Suggestions

Garlicky Kale (page 201)
Chickpea Croutons (page 222)
Coconut Quinoa (page 235)

Trim the stem of the cauliflower, while keeping the head intact. Hold the cauliflower with its base (stem end) on a cutting board. With a sharp knife, make one cut through the center to divide the cauliflower in half. Cut each half into 1¼-inch-thick slices. There should be 3 or 4 "steaks" in total. Cut the remaining cauliflower into bite-size florets.

Make the batter by adding the vegan buttermilk to the flour mixture. Mix well to combine until smooth.

Add enough neutral oil to cover the base of a large nonstick skillet to a depth of about ⅓ inch. Heat the oil over medium-high heat until shimmering.

Meanwhile, dip one of the cauliflower steaks into the batter, letting any excess drip off. Then dip the steak into the panko until fully coated. Using tongs, place the cauliflower steak into the shimmering oil. Repeat for each steak, placing them in a single layer in the skillet. Cook for about 3 minutes on each side, or until golden brown. Transfer the steaks to the prepared baking sheet.

Place the florets onto a separate baking sheet and drizzle with olive oil to coat. Sprinkle generously with salt. Use your hands to rub the florets with the olive oil and salt until they are evenly coated.

Place the cauliflower steaks on the top rack of the oven, and the florets on the rack below. Roast the steaks for 5 minutes. Flip the steaks over and roast for about 2 minutes more, or until they are fork-tender. Roast the florets for about 15 minutes, or until they are just tender.

Make the pimiento sauce: Meanwhile, drain the almonds and transfer them to a high-speed blender. Add the pimientos, garlic, lemon juice, mustard, sriracha, onion powder, smoked paprika, nutritional yeast, and 1½ cups water. Blend on high until smooth. Transfer the sauce to a medium saucepan and heat over medium heat for about 2 minutes, or until warmed through. Season with salt and pepper.

Drizzle a generous amount of the pimiento sauce on the steaks when serving. Use some of the remaining sauce to coat the roasted cauliflower florets. (Refrigerate any remaining sauce in an airtight container for up to 3 days.)

Braised Jackfruit Stew

1 (14-ounce) can **young jackfruit** packed in water and sea salt, drained and rinsed

2 tablespoons **olive oil**

3 tablespoons plus 3 cups **vegetable broth**

½ medium **yellow onion**, diced

3 **garlic cloves**, minced

2 tablespoons **tomato paste**

1 small **russet potato**, peeled and cut into ¾-inch pieces (about 1 cup)

1 large **carrot**, cut into ¾-inch-thick rounds (about ⅔ cup)

¾ teaspoon **smoked paprika**

½ teaspoon **chili powder**

½ teaspoon **onion powder**

½ teaspoon **dried oregano**

¼ teaspoon **crushed red pepper**

1 tablespoon **vegan Worcestershire sauce**

1 **bay leaf**

3 sprigs **fresh thyme**

½ cup halved **cherry tomatoes**

1½ teaspoons **flax meal** (ground flaxseeds)

Salt and freshly ground black pepper to taste

1½ tablespoons chopped **fresh parsley**, for garnish

This was the final recipe I tested for this cookbook. When I tasted it, I felt I had made a dish so hearty and meaty that even true meat lovers would enjoy it. That's my primary goal in writing the book: to get vegans and non-vegans to enjoy plant-based meals. And this recipe, for me, does exactly that. I hope you enjoy it as much as I do.

To reduce the cooking time, you can skip the first part of sautéing the jackfruit and instead add it directly to the saucepan with the carrots and potatoes. It will no longer technically be a "braised" stew, but it will still be a delicious stew. The reason for sautéing the jackfruit on its own is to add another layer of flavor from both the browning of the jackfruit and the fond (browned bits) left in the pan, which then go into the stew. But this is more of a culinary luxury than a necessity.

Be sure to buy young, or green, jackfruit packed in water and sea salt, and not ripe jackfruit. The brand I like is Native Forest.

Serve your jackfruit stew with a simple side of steamed rice or a different grain of your choice. Additional serving suggestions are listed on page 170.

Serves 3

Dry the jackfruit well using paper towels. Heat 1 tablespoon of the oil in a medium nonstick saucepan or Dutch oven over medium-high heat. Transfer the jackfruit to the pot, spreading out the pieces. Cook the jackfruit for 8 to 10 minutes, until golden brown on each side, stirring occasionally. Transfer the jackfruit to a plate.

Add 3 tablespoons of the vegetable broth to the saucepan and deglaze the pan with a wooden spoon, scraping the browned bits stuck to the bottom and sides of the pan.

Reduce the heat to medium and add the remaining tablespoon of olive oil. Cook the onion for about 5 minutes, or until the onion is translucent. Add the garlic and cook for 30 seconds more. Add the tomato paste and cook for 2 minutes, stirring constantly. Add the potato, carrot, smoked paprika, chili powder, onion powder, oregano, and crushed red pepper and cook for 30 seconds, stirring constantly.

Recipe continues

Other Serving Suggestions

Garlicky Kale (page 201)
Garlicky Rice (page 235)
Coconut Quinoa (page 235)
Lemony Cauliflower Rice
  (page 237)
Cheesy Savory Pancakes
  (page 239)
Cornbread Mug Cake (page 244)

Add the remaining 3 cups vegetable broth, along with the Worcestershire sauce, bay leaf, thyme, cherry tomatoes, and jackfruit. Bring the liquid to a boil, then reduce the heat. Cover and simmer for 25 to 30 minutes, until the potatoes and carrots are tender, stirring every 10 minutes or so.

Remove the bay leaf and thyme. Add the flax meal and stir for 30 seconds.

Using the side of a spatula, shred the jackfruit into smaller pieces. Season with salt and pepper. Garnish with parsley and serve.

London Broil Tempeh with Smashed Potatoes

6 medium Yukon Gold potatoes, washed, peeled, and halved lengthwise

Salt

2 (8-ounce) packages tempeh

Marinade

⅓ cup low-sodium tamari or soy sauce

1½ tablespoons vegan Worcestershire sauce

1½ tablespoons olive oil

1 tablespoon plus 2 teaspoons maple syrup

2 teaspoons freshly squeezed lemon juice

¾ teaspoon minced fresh garlic

¾ teaspoon minced fresh ginger

4 tablespoons vegan butter

½ cup thinly sliced green onions (about 6 green onions, green parts only)

¼ cup unsweetened nondairy milk, preferably oat milk

1 teaspoon garlic powder

Ground white pepper

I spent several years of my childhood in England. Most of the comfort foods there involved some variety of meat with potatoes. This dish provides that same comfort, but without the meat.

Tempeh is a healthful protein-rich meat substitute, and its firm texture makes it particularly well-suited for this dish. Unlike meat, tempeh is rich in fiber, and contains zero cholesterol.

The marinade has a powerful umami flavor from the vegan Worcestershire sauce and packs a punch with the fresh ginger and garlic.

This recipe calls for the optional step of simmering the tempeh prior to slicing. I highly recommend taking this extra step as it removes the slightly bitter flavor. It also softens the tempeh, allowing it to absorb more of the marinade.

The tempeh is served with a generous portion of smashed potatoes for a hearty, "stick to your ribs" dinner.

Serves 4

Place the potatoes in a medium saucepan with enough cold water to cover by about 2 inches. Bring the water to a gentle boil before adding 1 teaspoon salt. Cover the saucepan and cook the potatoes for about 20 minutes, or until a knife can be inserted into the middle of a potato with almost no resistance. Keep an eye on the potatoes to avoid overcooking them. Drain the potatoes and place them back into the hot saucepan for 1 minute to remove excess moisture. Transfer to a large bowl.

Meanwhile, preheat the oven to 450°F. Line a baking sheet with parchment paper or a silicone mat. Set aside.

In a medium saucepan, bring enough water to cover the tempeh by about 2 inches to a boil. Add the tempeh and reduce the heat. Simmer for 3 minutes. Drain the tempeh and pat it dry. Set aside to cool.

Make the marinade: In a medium bowl, mix the tamari, Worcestershire, olive oil, maple syrup, lemon juice, garlic, and ginger.

Recipe continues

Slice each block of tempeh into 8 equal-sized rectangles, for a total of 16 rectangles (see page 36). Lay the rectangles in a single layer in a medium baking dish. Pour the marinade over the top of the rectangles and use your hands to rub them with the marinade. Set aside for at least 10 minutes.

Meanwhile, pass the potatoes through a ricer into a large bowl (my favorite method), or mash them with a potato masher. Set aside.

Transfer the tempeh to the prepared baking sheet, reserving the leftover marinade. Roast the tempeh for 10 minutes. Flip the rectangles over and roast for another 5 to 7 minutes, until they start to brown. Turn on the oven broiler and broil for about 2 minutes more, or until they start to become crispy.

Meanwhile, melt the butter in a small skillet over medium-low heat. Add the green onions and cook for 1 to 2 minutes, until they start to become tender. Add the nondairy milk and cook until warmed through. Transfer the milk mixture to the bowl with the potatoes. Add the garlic powder and ¼ teaspoon white pepper. Stir to combine. (Avoid overmixing or else you will end up with gummy potatoes.) Season with more salt and white pepper if necessary.

Heat the remaining marinade in a small saucepan and pour over the cooked tempeh. Serve with smashed potatoes.

Chickpea Cashew Loaf with Ketchup

1 teaspoon plus 1 tablespoon **olive oil**

1 large **yellow onion**, diced

2 medium **carrots**, finely diced

2 **celery stalks**, finely diced

4 **garlic cloves**, minced

1 cup **raw cashews**, roughly chopped

Salt

1 teaspoon **dried thyme**

1 teaspoon **dried rosemary**

1 teaspoon **paprika**

¼ teaspoon **finely ground black pepper**

2 (15-ounce) cans **chickpeas**, drained and rinsed, or 3 cups cooked chickpeas

1¼ cups **dried bread crumbs**

¼ cup **low-sodium tamari or soy sauce**

2 tablespoons **tomato paste**

2 tablespoons **flax meal** (ground flaxseeds)

3 tablespoons **nutritional yeast**

Ketchup, store-bought or homemade (page 265; optional)

Move over, mushy lentil loaves. Chickpeas are a better vegan substitute for the meat in meat loaves, as they hold their texture even after being subjected to the whirling sharp blades of the food processor.

With protein and fiber from the chickpeas, healthy fats from the flax meal, and those essential Bs from the nutritional yeast, this is one nourishing loaf. (For a nut-free option, you can leave out the cashews.)

This loaf is so good with crispy potatoes and lots of ketchup. Use store-bought ketchup or make your own (page 265).

Serves 4

Preheat the oven to 375°F. Grease a nonstick 9 × 5-inch loaf pan with 1 teaspoon of the olive oil. Set aside.

Heat the remaining 1 tablespoon olive oil in a large skillet over medium-high heat. Add the onion, carrots, and celery and cook for about 5 minutes, or until the onion is translucent. Add the garlic and cook for another 30 seconds.

Add the cashews, ¼ teaspoon salt, the thyme, rosemary, paprika, and black pepper and continue cooking for 1 minute more.

Transfer the mixture to a large bowl. Add the chickpeas, bread crumbs, tamari, tomato paste, flax meal, and nutritional yeast. Use your hands to fully incorporate the ingredients. Add salt to taste.

Transfer the chickpea mixture in batches to a food processor and pulse until about half of the chickpeas are mashed, leaving the remaining chickpeas whole. The mixture should hold together but still have some texture.

Transfer the mixture to the prepared loaf pan. Smooth it evenly and press down on the mixture, making sure to get it as flat and even as possible.

Bake the loaf for 30 minutes.

Serve the loaf with ketchup, if desired, on the side.

Chickpea & Sun-Dried Tomato Coconut Stew

2 teaspoons neutral cooking oil (see page 18)

1 small yellow onion, chopped

½ cup sun-dried tomatoes, chopped

3 large garlic cloves, minced

1 tablespoon minced fresh ginger

Zest of ½ lemon

½ teaspoon paprika

1 (15-ounce) can chickpeas, drained and rinsed, or 1½ cups cooked chickpeas

1 (5-ounce) package baby spinach

1 (14-ounce) can unsweetened coconut milk

1 tablespoon freshly squeezed lemon juice

Salt and freshly ground black pepper to taste

This uniquely flavored stew combines the sweet-tart quality of sun-dried tomatoes with creamy coconut. Tangy and divine!

Not only is this a restaurant-quality meal, it's also a balanced one. There are chickpeas for protein, spinach for some greens, and your choice of grain. Did I mention that this is a one-pot dish? Which translates to very little cleanup. Just the way we like it!

So, what exactly are sun-dried tomatoes? They are tomatoes that have had their moisture removed through a long drying process that thickens their skins, helping to prevent bacteria and microorganisms from entering and spoiling them. Besides extending their shelf life, the drying process also concentrates their flavor, making them even more delicious. And if that's not enough, they are rich in vitamins, minerals, and antioxidants, particularly lycopene, which is a powerful antioxidant. They are sold either dried in packets or soaked in oil. For this recipe, use the jarred sun-dried tomatoes that come in olive oil if they're available at your supermarket. Otherwise, any jarred or canned variety will work. Do not used dried.

Serve your stew with a simple side of steamed rice or a different grain of your choice. Additional serving suggestions are listed on the opposite page.

Serves 2 to 3

Heat the oil in a large saucepan over medium heat. Add the onion and cook for about 6 minutes, or until it starts to brown. Reduce the heat to medium-low and add the sun-dried tomatoes, garlic, ginger, lemon zest, and paprika. Cook for 3 minutes more, stirring constantly.

Add the chickpeas and cook for about 5 minutes, stirring frequently, or until lightly browned. Add 3 tablespoons water and deglaze the pan with a wooden spoon, scraping the browned bits stuck to the bottom and sides of the saucepan.

Add the spinach, 1 cup at a time. Cook each cup, stirring, until wilted, before adding the next cup.

Then add the coconut milk and stir to combine. Reduce the heat to low and simmer for about 5 minutes, or until the coconut milk is warmed through. Add the lemon juice, salt, and pepper and serve.

Other Serving Suggestions

Garlicky Rice (page 235)
Coconut Quinoa (page 235)
Lemony Cauliflower Rice (page 237)

Inverted Ratatouille

2 medium-large eggplant (about 1 pound each)

6 tablespoons plus 2 teaspoons olive oil

Salt and freshly ground black pepper

3 large garlic cloves, minced

½ teaspoon smoked paprika

½ teaspoon onion powder

½ teaspoon dried oregano

⅛ teaspoon cayenne pepper

⅛ teaspoon chipotle powder

1 (14.5-ounce) can diced tomatoes

1 teaspoon Dijon mustard

1 teaspoon maple syrup

1 (15-ounce) can chickpeas, drained and rinsed, or 1½ cups cooked chickpeas

1 cup chopped kale leaves

¼ cup vegetable broth or water, plus more as needed

Standard ratatouille is made with tomatoes, sautéed garlic, onion, zucchini, eggplant, bell peppers, and herbes de Provence. My faux ratatouille omits the zucchini and bell peppers, replaces the onion with onion powder, includes chickpeas for protein, and uses eggplant as a bed for the sauce. It also uses Mexican spices instead of Provençal seasoning. So maybe it's nothing like ratatouille. Except that it reminds me of ratatouille and does have several similarities.

Name aside, this combination is delicious and gorgeous. In Instagram lingo, this dish is pure "vegan foodporn"! Save this one for a dinner party, or for when you're cooking for friends. They'll be very impressed.

Serves 3 to 4

Preheat the oven to 425°F. Line a baking sheet with parchment paper or a silicone mat. Set aside.

Cut the eggplant in half lengthwise. Score the cut sides of both eggplant using the tip of a small knife. Make small incisions in a crosshatch pattern on all 4 halves without piercing the skin. Drizzle 1½ tablespoons of the olive oil evenly over the cut side of each half, making sure the oil gets into the incisions. Rub the olive oil into the flesh. Season generously with salt and pepper. Place the eggplant, cut side down, on the prepared baking sheet and roast for about 30 minutes, or until a knife can be inserted into the middle meeting almost no resistance. Remove the eggplant from the oven and turn them cut side up.

Meanwhile, heat the remaining 2 teaspoons olive oil in a medium saucepan over medium-low heat. Add the garlic and cook for 30 seconds. Add the smoked paprika, onion powder, oregano, cayenne, and chipotle powder and cook for 30 seconds more, stirring constantly. Add the diced tomatoes, mustard, and maple syrup. Bring the tomatoes to a simmer and add the chickpeas, kale, and vegetable broth. Continue to simmer until the kale is just wilted and the chickpeas are warmed through. Add more vegetable broth if the sauce becomes too dry. Season with salt and black pepper.

Use your hands to gently pull apart the squares of the eggplant to allow the sauce to run in between the cuts. Pour a quarter of the chickpea tomato sauce over each half. Serve immediately.

Chickpea Nuggets with Crispy Oven Fries

We didn't have fast-food restaurants in Jamaica when I was a child, but I was fortunate to get the real deal from my grandma. She made the best chicken nuggets and french fries I have ever eaten. She was so skilled at getting them perfectly crispy, all the while humming Bob Marley tunes.

I have created two plant-based versions and couldn't decide which one to share with you, so I'm giving you both awesome nugget recipes, Chickpea Nuggets and Tempeh Nuggets (page 219)—each crispy and loaded with plant-based protein and yet totally different in taste. I'm spoiling you, friends. Enjoy!

This recipe makes it easy to prepare your fries and chickpea nuggets at the same time, so they are both perfectly crispy for serving. Don't worry if your timing doesn't go quite as planned, both nuggets and fries can be reheated in a 400°F oven for 5 to 10 minutes.

Serves 2 (makes 12 nuggets)

Crispy Oven Fries

2 medium **russet potatoes**, peeled or unpeeled, cut into ¼ × ¼-inch strips of equal length

1 to 1½ tablespoons **olive oil**, as needed

Salt to taste

Chickpea Nuggets

1 cup **old-fashioned rolled oats**

1 (15-ounce) can **chickpeas**, or 1½ cups cooked chickpeas plus ¼ cup cooking liquid

¾ teaspoon **onion powder**

¾ teaspoon **garlic power**

¾ teaspoon **smoked paprika**

¾ teaspoon **chili powder**

1 tablespoon **olive oil**

Salt

Prepare the crispy oven fries: Rinse the potato strips until the water runs clear. Transfer them to a large bowl with enough water to cover by about 2 inches. Soak for 30 minutes.

Preheat the oven to 375°F. Line a large baking sheet with parchment paper or a silicone mat. Set aside.

Make the chickpea nuggets: Pulse the rolled oats in a food processor until they are ground into a coarse, powder-like consistency. Transfer to a small bowl and set aside.

Drain the chickpeas, reserving ¼ cup of the liquid from the can. Rinse the chickpeas. Transfer them to a food processor with the onion powder, garlic powder, smoked paprika, and chili powder. Pulse for about 15 seconds, or until the chickpeas are crumbly in texture. (Be careful not to pulse the chickpeas too much. We are not making hummus!)

Transfer the crumbled chickpea mixture to a large bowl. Add the ¼ cup reserved liquid, the olive oil, and ground oats. Mix well to incorporate all the ingredients. Add ½ teaspoon salt and adjust to taste. Let the nugget batter rest for 10 minutes.

Recipe continues

Practically Vegan

While the batter is resting, drain the potato strips. Dry them thoroughly using a kitchen towel or paper towel. In a large bowl, toss them with just enough olive oil to coat and a generous dash of salt. Transfer them to the prepared baking sheet in an even single layer without touching. Bake for 20 minutes.

While the fries are baking, line a separate large baking sheet with parchment paper or a silicone mat. Using 2 tablespoons of the batter for each nugget and your hands, form them into the desired shape. Place the nuggets on the prepared baking sheet in a single layer, also not touching.

Once the fries have baked for 20 minutes, remove them from the oven and toss so they cook evenly on all sides. Increase the oven temperature to 425°F. Bake the fries for about 20 minutes more, or until golden brown.

Bake the nuggets at the same time as the fries at 425°F for 15 minutes. Flip them over and bake for another 8 to 10 minutes, until they are crispy and golden brown.

Salt the fries to taste once they are done cooking. Serve immediately with the chickpea nuggets when they are done.

Sloppy Joes

2 cups **dried green lentils**, rinsed

2 tablespoons **olive oil**

1 medium **yellow onion**, diced small

3 **garlic cloves**, minced

½ teaspoon **ground coriander**

½ teaspoon **dried thyme**

½ teaspoon **dried oregano**

½ teaspoon **chili powder**

½ teaspoon **paprika**

¼ teaspoon **ground cumin**

¼ teaspoon **celery seed** (optional)

Cracked black pepper

2 tablespoons **vegan Worcestershire sauce**

2 tablespoons **maple syrup**

1½ tablespoons **coconut aminos,** or low-sodium **tamari** or **soy sauce**

1 (15-ounce) can **tomato sauce**

For Serving (Optional)

8 **hot dog buns**

Cabbage Slaw (page 191)

You know that feeling when you've hit a home run? These sandwiches gave me that feeing the first time I made them. As soon as I sank my teeth into one of these saucy sloppy joes, I knew they were going to be a hit. And they were. My family devoured them without coming up for air. (By the way, I've never played baseball, so I don't actually know what hitting a home run feels like.)

I recommend serving your joes with my Cabbage Slaw (page 191), but I'll leave that up to you.

And if you're not into the whole bun thing, these sloppy lentils are so good you can even eat them solo. Or pair them with a grain of your choice. They're also yummy with pasta or potatoes.

One more thing before I leave you to enjoy your saucy buns. Lentils happen to be loaded with protein, and you'd be surprised at how many lentils you can fit into a hot dog bun! Getting enough protein on a plant-based diet is much easier than you might think.

Serves 4 (makes 8 buns)

Add the lentils to a medium saucepan with 4 cups water. Bring the water to a boil. Reduce the heat to a gentle simmer, cover, and cook your lentils for about 20 minutes, or until al dente. Add more water as needed to keep the lentils submerged. Drain and set aside.

Meanwhile, heat the olive oil in a large sauté pan over medium heat. Add the onion and cook for 5 to 7 minutes, until translucent. Add the garlic, coriander, thyme, oregano, chili powder, paprika, cumin, celery seed (if using), and a few turns of pepper and cook for 1 minute more, stirring constantly.

Stir in the Worcestershire, maple syrup, and coconut aminos. Add the tomato sauce and cooked lentils. Stir and simmer for about 5 minutes, or until the sauce has thickened and is warmed through.

Meanwhile, if desired, warm the buns in a 350°F oven or toaster oven for about 5 minutes, or until they are warmed through and lightly crispy. Add the desired quantity of saucy lentils to each bun. Serve with a side of slaw, if using.

Cauliflower, Lentil & Mushroom Stew

2 tablespoons **vegan butter**

1 (8-ounce) package **baby bella (cremini) or white button mushrooms**, stems trimmed, roughly chopped

1 large **yellow onion**, diced small

1 tablespoon **olive oil**

5 **garlic cloves**, minced

1 **serrano pepper**, minced and seeded

1 tablespoon finely chopped **fresh rosemary**

⅓ cup **tomato paste**

3 cups **frozen riced cauliflower**, thawed

¾ cup **red lentils**, rinsed (see page 39)

3 cups **vegetable broth**, plus more as needed

1 tablespoon **vegan Worcestershire sauce**

Zest of ½ **lemon**

1 tablespoon **freshly squeezed lemon juice**, or to taste

Salt and freshly ground black pepper to taste

3 tablespoons chopped **fresh parsley**

This cozy stew can double as a soup simply by adding more vegetable broth. I sometimes eat it as a stew with rice or quinoa, and other times, I add a cup or two more broth and enjoy it as a soup on its own.

I tend to buy frozen riced cauliflower rather than make my own. It's quite time consuming to make, and with the frozen stuff so widely available, why go through all that trouble? I'd rather spend my time coming up with recipes!

Enjoy your stew with a simple side of steamed rice or a different grain of your choice. Garlicky Rice (page 235) and Coconut Quinoa (page 235) would also pair well with this recipe.

Serves 4 to 5

Melt the butter in a large saucepan or Dutch oven over medium-high heat. Add the mushrooms and cook for 4 to 6 minutes, until they are golden brown.

Add the onion and olive oil and cook for 6 to 8 minutes, stirring occasionally, until the onion is golden brown. Reduce the heat to medium and add the garlic, serrano, and rosemary and cook for 3 minutes, stirring constantly.

Add the tomato paste and cook for 2 more minutes, stirring constantly.

Stir in the cauliflower rice, red lentils, vegetable broth, and Worcestershire. Bring the liquid to a boil, then reduce the heat to a simmer, cover, and cook for 15 to 20 minutes, until the lentils are tender. Stir frequently and add more vegetable broth as needed.

Remove the pan from the heat and mix in the lemon zest and juice, adding more lemon juice to taste. Season with salt and pepper. Garnish with parsley and serve.

Mushroom Bourguignon

1 tablespoon olive oil

1 small yellow onion, diced

1 (8-ounce) package baby bella (cremini) or white button mushrooms, stems trimmed, halved

Salt

¼ cup red wine

3 large garlic cloves, minced

2 medium carrots, sliced into ¾-inch-thick rounds (about 1 cup)

1 medium red bell pepper, cut into ½-inch pieces

2 large celery stalks, sliced into ¼-inch-thick half-moons (about ¾ cup)

1 tablespoon fresh thyme leaves, or 1 teaspoon dried thyme

2 teaspoons finely chopped fresh rosemary

¼ teaspoon garlic powder

¼ teaspoon finely ground black pepper

1 tablespoon tomato paste

1 tablespoon low-sodium tamari or soy sauce

½ cup vegetable broth or water

1 tablespoon cornstarch or arrowroot

Freshly ground black pepper to taste

Bourguignon refers to a recipe prepared in the style of the French region of Bourgogne (known as Burgundy in English). Perhaps the best known recipe prepared in the bourguignon style is beef bourguignon, or beef braised in red wine. I substituted the chunks of beef with large pieces of mushrooms for this vegan version.

This dish works well with a side that can sop up the yummy sauce in the stew. My go-to is the Smashed Potatoes (page 227). Noodles and crispy toast also pair well with this dish.

Serves 2 to 3

Heat the olive oil in a large saucepan or Dutch oven over medium-high heat. Add the onion, mushrooms, and a pinch of salt and cook for about 4 minutes, or until the onion starts to brown.

Add the red wine and cook for 10 seconds more, stirring frequently.

Stir in the garlic, carrots, bell pepper, celery, thyme, rosemary, garlic powder, and the finely ground black pepper and cook for 1 minute.

Add the tomato paste and cook for 2 minutes more, stirring constantly.

Add the tamari and vegetable broth and bring to a boil. Reduce the heat to a simmer, cover, and cook for 12 to 15 minutes, until the carrots are just fork-tender.

In a small bowl, mix the cornstarch with 3 tablespoons water to make a slurry. Add the slurry to the stew and mix well to incorporate. Cook for about 1 minute more while stirring, or until the sauce thickens. Season with salt and black pepper.

Chapter 7

Sides

This is where the magic begins. The following recipes are broken down into three categories: Salads & Veggie Sides, Protein Sides, and Potato Sides & Starchy Sides. Mix and match these recipes to create your own delicious plant-based bowls. Ideally, you want to try and have some combination of veggies, protein, and starch in your bowl, along with some healthy fats from the dip, dressing, or sauce (see pages 249–265) you choose. But if you are really craving a bowl of four types of potatoes, go for it. Have fun and grow your love for plant-based food.

These sides are also delicious accompaniments to the mains in this cookbook.

Cabbage Slaw

This quick and delicious slaw is ideal for adding some crunch and extra flavor to sandwiches, wraps, and burgers. It's made with an Asian-inspired dressing that's just the right amount of sweet and tangy, with a hint of sesame.

Serves 3

Dressing

2 tablespoons **freshly squeezed lime juice**

2 teaspoons **rice vinegar**

2 teaspoons **tamari or soy sauce**

2 teaspoons **maple syrup**

1½ teaspoons **toasted sesame oil**

1 (¼-inch) piece **fresh ginger**

1 **garlic clove**

Salad

½ small head **green cabbage**, tough outer leaves and core discarded, thinly sliced (about 3 cups)

2 medium **carrots**, grated (about 1 cup)

4 **green onions** (green parts only), thinly sliced (about ⅓ cup)

¼ cup **raw pepitas** (shelled pumpkin seeds) **or** roughly chopped **raw cashews** (optional)

Salt and freshly ground black pepper to taste

Make the dressing: In a small bowl, mix the lime juice, vinegar, tamari, maple syrup, and toasted sesame oil. Grate the ginger and garlic directly into the bowl using a Microplane or fine grater. Stir to combine. Set aside.

Make the salad: In a large bowl, combine the cabbage, carrots, green onions, and pepitas (if using). Add the dressing and mix well. Season with salt and pepper.

Mediterranean-Inspired Salad

3 large **Roma tomatoes**, cut into ¾-inch pieces (about 2 cups)

1 **English cucumber**, cut into ¾-inch pieces (about 1 cup)

⅓ cup pitted and sliced **kalamata olives**

1 medium **avocado**, cut into ¾-inch pieces (about 1 cup)

½ (15-ounce) can **chickpeas**, drained and rinsed, or ¾ cup cooked chickpeas

¼ cup **extra-virgin olive oil**

1 teaspoon **lemon pepper seasoning**, or ½ teaspoon **lemon zest**, ⅛ teaspoon **finely ground black pepper**, and ¼ teaspoon **salt**

1 tablespoon plus 1 teaspoon **freshly squeezed lemon juice**

1 small **garlic clove**

Salt to taste

½ cup chopped **fresh parsley**

This simple salad has a lot going for it: vitamin C and lycopene (a strong antioxidant) from the tomatoes, good fats from the avocado and olives, plant protein from the chickpeas, plus lots of flavor from the fresh parsley and lemon pepper. Lemon pepper is a very versatile seasoning that's easy to find. It adds a zingy, peppery flavor to marinades and salad dressings. It's also easy to substitute if you don't have any on hand (see ingredients).

I like to add garlic to dressings, guacamole, and salsa by grating it with a Microplane or fine grater. This method distributes the garlic more evenly, making the dish extra flavorful.

Serves 3

Place the tomatoes, cucumber, olives, avocado, and chickpeas in a large bowl. Set aside.

In a small bowl, combine the olive oil, lemon pepper, and lemon juice. Finely grate the garlic clove directly into the bowl using a Microplane or fine grater. Whisk to combine. Season with salt.

Transfer the dressing to the bowl with the salad. Sprinkle the parsley on top, mix to combine, and season with salt.

Kale Caesar Salad with Chickpeas

Chickpeas

1 (15-ounce) can chickpeas, drained, and rinsed, or 1½ cups cooked chickpeas

1 tablespoon neutral cooking oil (see page 18)

¼ teaspoon crushed red pepper

Salt

6 cups chopped curly kale (about 1 medium bunch, tough stems removed)

Vegan Caesar Salad Dressing (page 258)

Salt

Traditional Caesar salad—made with anchovy fillets, egg yolks, and Parmesan—is far from being vegan. In this recipe, seaweed flakes (or granules) and vegan Worcestershire sauce are used in place of the anchovies, nutritional yeast in place of Parmesan, and cashews to mimic the creamy texture of the egg yolks. Add a pinch of kala namak for more of an eggy flavor if you happen to have some.

I included the chickpeas as a source of protein and to add a delicious crunch.

Serves 4

Prepare the chickpeas: Dry the chickpeas by placing them between paper towels or a folded dish towel and rubbing them back and forth. (You can also remove the skins at this point.)

Heat the oil in a large skillet over medium-high heat. Once the oil starts to shimmer, add the chickpeas and crushed red pepper. Sauté the chickpeas for about 5 minutes, or until golden brown. Transfer the chickpeas, using a slotted spoon, to a plate lined with paper towels. Season with a dash of salt. Set aside.

Transfer the chopped kale to a large bowl. Add the dressing. Massage the kale with the dressing for about 3 minutes, or until the leaves soften. Add the chickpeas and mix well to combine. Season with salt.

Asian-Inspired Crunchy Salad with Sesame Ginger Dressing

This salad is substantial enough to be a main dish. (For a lighter, equally delicious version, you can leave the tofu out.) I like to cut the tofu into strips that resemble the shapes of the sliced veggies. The strips get tossed with cornstarch, which makes them nice and crispy when they're baked or sautéed. Both stovetop and oven (oil-free) cooking methods are provided below.

The tangy sesame ginger dressing is the icing on the cake—or salad, in this case. Do make sure to take the time to massage the kale with the dressing. It softens the kale and gives it a better texture for salads.

Serves 5

1 (14-ounce) block **extra-firm tofu**, pressed and cut into ¼ × 1½-inch strips or ¾-inch cubes (see page 34)

1 tablespoon **cornstarch**

1 teaspoon **garlic powder**

Salt

1 tablespoon **sesame oil or neutral cooking oil** (see page 18; optional)

6 cups chopped **curly kale**, (about 1 medium bunch, tough stems removed)

2 cups julienned **carrots** (about 3 medium carrots)

¼ medium head **purple cabbage**, tough outer leaves and core discarded, thinly sliced (about 2 cups)

⅓ cup thinly sliced **green onions** (green parts only; about 4 green onions)

Sesame Ginger Salad Dressing (page 257)

¼ cup **peanuts**, roughly chopped (optional)

Freshly ground black pepper to taste

Prepare the tofu: Place the tofu into a large plastic zip-top bag or airtight container. In a small bowl, combine the cornstarch, garlic powder, and ¼ teaspoon salt and mix well. Transfer the cornstarch mixture to the zip-top bag and gently rotate the bag, moving the tofu around until all the pieces are coated with the cornstarch.

Cooking method 1: Heat the sesame oil in a large skillet over medium-high heat. Add the tofu and sauté for about 10 minutes, or until all sides are golden brown. (You may have to do this in batches to avoid overcrowding the pan. The tofu should be in a single layer. You will need to toss the tofu to make sure all sides brown.)

Cooking method 2 *(oil-free):* Preheat the oven to 400°F. Line a large baking sheet with parchment paper or a silicone mat. Place the tofu on the prepared baking sheet in a single layer. Bake for 10 minutes. Toss the tofu and bake for 5 to 10 minutes more, until golden brown.

Make the salad: In a large bowl, combine the kale, carrots, cabbage, and green onions. Add the dressing to the bowl. Use your hands to massage the veggies with the dressing, especially the kale, for about 3 minutes, or until the kale softens.

Add the tofu and peanuts (if using) and toss to combine. Season with salt and pepper.

Roasted Broccoli or Cauliflower Bites

My youngest daughter, Asha, has a knack for making the most delicious vegetables. Her recipes bring out the best qualities of the vegetable while still maintaining its integrity. She has a deep respect for nature (including mosquitoes!), and when I watch her making her vegetable dishes, I notice she maintains this same respect. Thank you, Asha, for this simple yet delicious recipe.

Serves 3

6 large **garlic cloves**, minced

3 tablespoons **olive oil**

3 tablespoons **coconut aminos**

1 small to medium head **broccoli or cauliflower**, cut into bite-size florets (about 4 cups)

Salt to taste

Preheat the oven to 400°F.

In a small bowl, mix the garlic, olive oil, and coconut aminos to make a marinade.

Dry the broccoli thoroughly using a kitchen towel or paper towel. Transfer the broccoli to a large plastic zip-top bag. Add the marinade. Squeeze out the air while sealing the bag. Toss the broccoli until it is fully coated with the marinade. Transfer the broccoli to a large rimmed baking sheet, making sure to transfer all the marinade and garlic from the bag.

Roast for about 15 minutes, or until the broccoli is cooked but still has a crunch. Transfer to a serving dish, making sure to get all the garlic and marinade onto the broccoli. Season with salt.

Sheet Pan Veggies with Tahini Dijon Dressing

2 cups **broccoli or broccolini florets**

2 cups halved medium to large **Brussels sprouts**

1 medium to large **sweet potato**, peeled, cut into 1-inch pieces (about 2 cups)

Olive oil, for roasting

Dash of **garlic powder**

Dash of **salt and freshly ground black pepper**

Tahini Dijon Dressing (page 260)

With just a single sheet pan to clean and an easy four-ingredient dressing to whip up—oh, and the twenty-minute cook time—this is bound to become one of your go-to sides.

You can switch out the veggies and use what you have on hand. Just make sure to use firmer veggies like cauliflower, carrots, bell peppers, and squash. Keep to the quantities and sizes of the veggies in the recipe. You can even add some chickpeas to the mix to get in that plant protein.

Serves 4

Preheat the oven to 400°F. Line a large baking sheet with parchment paper or a silicone mat. Set aside.

Combine the broccoli, Brussels sprouts, and sweet potato in a medium bowl. Toss with just enough olive oil to give the vegetables a slick, glossy coating. Add the garlic powder, salt, and black pepper and use your hands to rub the vegetables with the oil and seasonings.

Transfer the vegetables to the prepared baking sheet, placing them in a single layer without overcrowding. Roast for 15 minutes, then toss. Roast for about 5 minutes more, or until the sweet potato is just tender. If desired, change the oven setting to broil and cook for about 2 minutes more, or until the Brussels sprouts are slightly charred. Transfer the roasted vegetables to a large bowl.

Add the desired amount of dressing to the roasted vegetables and stir to coat. Refrigerate any remaining dressing in an airtight container for up to 5 days.

Garlicky Kale

1 medium bunch **curly kale** (about 7 stems)

2 tablespoons **olive oil**

4 **garlic cloves**, minced

1 teaspoon **coconut aminos**, plus more to taste

It's called mighty kale for a reason. This nutrient-loaded leafy green has reached celebrity status, displacing other greens in salads, soups, and pesto. There are even kale chips in the snack aisles.

Try to incorporate both cooked and raw kale into your diet, as both have slightly different health benefits.

Once you discover my favorite trio for cooking veggies—olive oil, garlic, and coconut aminos—and how effectively they can turn your veggies into a most scrumptious side, you'll want to use them over and over again. It's my go-to method for making my kids polish off their veggies. They literally eat bowlfuls of this stuff!

Just be sure to do a good job of removing the stem, as it can make your kale really tough—and not in the mighty way!

Serves 2

Tear the kale leaves into bite-size pieces and discard the stems. Set aside.

Heat the olive oil in a large sauté pan over medium heat. Cook the garlic, stirring constantly, for about 2 minutes, or until fragrant and softened. Be careful not to let it burn.

Add the kale, about 2 large handfuls at a time, stirring it with the garlic before adding more. Cook for 3 to 4 minutes, until the kale is wilted and bright green.

Add the coconut aminos, mix to combine, and adjust to taste.

Sautéed Asparagus with Garlic "Facon"

50 medium **asparagus spears** (about 2 pounds)

2 tablespoons **olive oil**

5 large **garlic cloves**, finely chopped

3 tablespoons **low-sodium soy sauce or tamari**

Salt and freshly ground black pepper to taste

I remember being reprimanded in culinary school for burning my garlic. It's a cooking faux pas. As it turns out, burning my garlic was actually not such a bad thing after all. When I was once too lazy to start over, I discovered that, by adding soy sauce to my slightly burnt garlic, it can be made to taste like bacon (or "facon" in vegan lingo). Obviously, it doesn't actually turn the garlic into bacon; it just makes it taste like bacon. Or at least what I remember bacon tasting like. Regardless, it's delicious.

None of my kids previously liked asparagus. That's until my youngest daughter, Asha, came up with the idea of combining it with garlic "facon."

Serves 5

Break off the woody ends of the asparagus by bending the spears near the base. It will snap in the right place. Discard the ends.

Heat the olive oil in a large skillet over medium-high heat. Add the garlic and cook for about 1 minute, or until it starts to turn slightly golden. Add the asparagus and soy sauce. Cook for another 6 to 7 minutes, stirring frequently, until the asparagus turns a darker green. Remove from the heat. Season with salt and pepper.

Creamy Miso Cauliflower

1 medium head cauliflower, chopped into bite-size florets (about 5 cups)

2 tablespoons olive oil

Dash of salt

Miso Cream Sauce

1 teaspoon mellow (white) miso

¾ cup raw cashews, soaked, drained, and rinsed (see page 39)

½ cup unsweetened nondairy milk

Zest of 1 small lemon

1½ tablespoons freshly squeezed lemon juice

¼ teaspoon apple cider vinegar

2½ tablespoons nutritional yeast

1 garlic clove

½ teaspoon garlic powder

¼ teaspoon onion powder

1 teaspoon salt, or to taste

Freshly ground black pepper to taste

Cauliflower is a nutrition superstar. Like broccoli, cabbage, Brussels sprouts, and kale, it's part of the cruciferous vegetable family. This family, a bit like mine because we eat so much fiber, has funny smelling sulfur-containing compounds. (They're called glucosinolates, if you're interested.) These compounds appear to have strong cancer-fighting capabilities.

Cauliflower is pretty much a blank slate in terms of taste and takes on the unique flavor of this sauce almost instantaneously, so combining it with this miso cream sauce is truly delicious.

Serves 4 to 5

Preheat the oven to 400°F.

Place the cauliflower florets into a large bowl. Add the olive oil and a generous dash of salt. Use your hands to coat the florets with the olive oil.

Transfer the cauliflower to a large baking sheet. Spread it out in a single layer and roast for about 15 minutes, or until just tender.

Meanwhile, make the miso cream sauce: In a small bowl, stir the miso into 2 teaspoons warm water until completely dissolved. Transfer the cashews, nondairy milk, lemon zest and juice, cider vinegar, nutritional yeast, garlic, garlic powder, onion powder, and dissolved miso into a high-speed blender. Blend on high until smooth.

Transfer the sauce from the blender to a large bowl. Stir in the roasted cauliflower until fully coated with the sauce. Season with the salt and pepper. Serve immediately.

Coconut-Battered Cauliflower Steaks

1 large head **cauliflower**, outer leaves removed

1 cup **all-purpose flour**

1 teaspoon **baking powder**

½ teaspoon **salt**

1 cup **unsweetened nondairy milk**

½ cup **shredded coconut**

Neutral cooking oil (see page 18), for pan-frying

Naya, my eldest daughter, actually ate one of these steaks for breakfast. She walked into the kitchen while I was testing the recipe, still in pajamas, and couldn't resist. Full disclosure: She is a teenager, so she gets up at noon!

When you cut your steaks, there will be some florets remaining. Cut them into bite-size pieces and save for another use. I usually toss them with a drizzle of olive oil, salt, and black pepper and roast them with the steaks, on a separate baking sheet, for about 20 minutes. They can also be added to chilis, curries, soups, and stews.

Serves 3 to 4

Preheat the oven to 400°F. Place an oven rack in the top position.

Trim the stem of the cauliflower while keeping the head intact. Hold the cauliflower with its base (stem end) on a cutting board. With a sharp knife, make one cut through the center to divide the cauliflower in half. Cut each half into ¾-inch-thick slices. There should be 3 or 4 steaks total.

In a wide bowl, whisk the flour, baking powder, and salt until combined. Add the nondairy milk and ¾ cup water, stirring until fully incorporated. Mix in the shredded coconut.

Add enough oil to cover the base of a large nonstick skillet to a depth of about ¼ inch. Heat the oil over medium-high heat until shimmering.

Meanwhile, dip one of the cauliflower steaks into the batter, shaking it to remove any excess. Place the cauliflower steak into the shimmering oil. (You can use a pair of tongs to do this.) Repeat for each steak, placing them in a single layer in the skillet. (You may need to do this in batches depending on the size of the skillet and the number of steaks.) Cook for about 5 minutes on each side, or until golden brown on both sides. Transfer the steaks to a baking sheet in a single layer.

Roast the steaks for 7 minutes on the top rack. Flip them over and roast for about 7 minutes more, or until just fork-tender at the thickest part. Serve immediately.

Roasted Carrots in Garlic-Chili Oil with Crunchy Pepitas

Pepitas (shelled pumpkin seeds) sautéed in homemade garlic-chili oil are not only divine, but they're also addictive. Roasted carrots get a complete facelift in this recipe. The combination of spicy, crunchy, salty, and sweet is just tantalizing.

One of the less talked-about benefits of carrots is that they can help alleviate constipation. That's because of their high fiber content. While this is primarily true of raw carrots, I thought it was worth sharing this interesting fact.

Serves 3

4 medium **carrots**, sliced into 2-inch coins, wider coins sliced in half (about 2 cups)

3 tablespoons **olive oil**

Salt

3 **garlic cloves**, finely minced

½ teaspoon **crushed red pepper**

¾ teaspoon **maple syrup**

2 tablespoons **raw pepitas** (shelled pumpkin seeds)

Preheat the oven to 425°F.

Place the carrots in a medium bowl and add 1 tablespoon of the olive oil and a generous dash of salt. Use your hands to toss the carrots in the oil and salt until evenly coated. Spread them out in a single layer on a large baking sheet. Roast for about 20 minutes, or until just fork-tender. (If you prefer softer carrots, cook to the desired tenderness.)

Meanwhile, heat the remaining 2 tablespoons olive oil in a medium skillet over medium heat. Once the oil starts sizzling, add the garlic and crushed red pepper and cook for about 30 seconds, or until fragrant. Stir constantly so the garlic does not burn. Transfer the garlic-chili oil to a small bowl. Add the maple syrup and mix to combine. Season with salt.

Once the carrots are done, transfer the flavored oil back to the skillet and add the roasted carrots and pepitas. Cook over medium-high heat for about 3 minutes, or until the pepitas are puffed and browned. Add salt to taste.

Maple Soy Green Beans

These saucy green beans will be gone in no time. The sautéed beans have just the right amount of crunch and soak up the tangy, slightly sweet, slightly spicy maple soy sauce delectably. The cornstarch slurry thickens the sauce a bit, so it sticks to the beans.

The maple soy sauce is very versatile and can be used with other veggies. It's a keeper!

Serves 4

Maple Soy Sauce

2 tablespoons coconut aminos

1 tablespoon low-sodium soy sauce or tamari

1 tablespoon maple syrup

2 teaspoons rice vinegar

½ teaspoon sriracha

1 teaspoon cornstarch

2 teaspoons sesame oil

8 ounces green beans, sliced into about 1½-inch pieces

2 garlic cloves, minced

¾ teaspoon minced fresh ginger

Make the maple soy sauce: In a small bowl, mix the coconut aminos, soy sauce, maple syrup, rice vinegar, and sriracha. Set aside.

In a separate small bowl, make a slurry by dissolving the cornstarch in 2 teaspoons water. Set aside.

Heat the sesame oil in a large skillet over medium-high heat. Add the green beans and sauté for about 4 minutes, or until they just become tender and start browning. Reduce the heat to medium-low. Move the green beans to the outer edge of the skillet and cook the garlic and ginger in the center for 30 seconds. Add the sauce and the slurry to the skillet and mix the garlic, ginger, and green beans into the sauce. Add 2 tablespoons water and mix. Cook for about 1 minute more, or until the sauce is warmed through and slightly thickened. Serve immediately.

Brussels Alfredo with Toasted Bread Crumbs

When my kids were younger, it was pretty impossible to get them to eat Brussels sprouts. I hated them, too, as a kid, because my British boarding school made the mushiest Brussels sprouts ever. I still cringe thinking about them.

When I came up with this recipe, Brussels sprouts quickly became a favorite in my house. When made this way, with creamy Alfredo sauce and garlicky bread crumbs, they're mighty hard to resist.

Serves 4

1 pound **Brussels sprouts**, trimmed and halved lengthwise

1 tablespoon plus 2 teaspoons **olive oil**

Dash of **salt**

3 **garlic cloves**, minced

¼ cup **dried bread crumbs**

½ teaspoon **crushed red pepper**

Alfredo Sauce

1 tablespoon **mellow (white) miso**

½ cup **raw cashews**, soaked, drained, and rinsed (see page 39)

2 tablespoons **cornstarch**

1 **garlic clove**, chopped

1 teaspoon **freshly squeezed lemon juice**

¼ teaspoon **sriracha**

¼ teaspoon **ground mustard seed**

Salt and freshly ground black pepper to taste

Preheat the oven to 425°F.

Place the halved Brussels sprouts in a large bowl. Add 1 tablespoon of the olive oil and the salt. Use your hands to rub the olive oil and salt onto the Brussels sprouts. Transfer them to a large baking sheet, spreading them out in a single layer, and roast for about 15 minutes, or until browned. Remove from the oven and set aside.

Meanwhile, heat the remaining 2 teaspoons olive oil in a large skillet over medium heat. Add the garlic and cook for 30 seconds, stirring constantly. Stir in the bread crumbs and crushed red pepper and cook for about 3 minutes more, or until the bread crumbs turn golden brown, stirring constantly. Set aside.

Make the Alfredo sauce: In a small bowl, stir the miso into 2 tablespoons warm water until completely dissolved.

Combine the cashews, cornstarch, dissolved miso, garlic, lemon juice, sriracha, ground mustard, and ¾ cup hot water in a high-speed blender. Blend on high until smooth.

Pour the Alfredo sauce into a small saucepan and cook over low heat for about 30 seconds, or until the sauce starts to thicken, whisking constantly. Remove from the heat and season with salt and pepper.

Transfer the roasted Brussels sprouts to a large serving bowl. Add the Alfredo sauce. Stir to combine. Gently fold in half of the toasted bread crumbs until evenly distributed. Season with salt. Top with the remaining toasted bread crumbs for serving. Serve immediately.

Easy Cheesy Nooch-Crusted Tofu

What is "nooch"? It's vegan slang for nutritional yeast. I discovered that nooch makes the most delicious cheesy crust, and it's loaded with those essential B vitamins.

This is one of my favorite tofu recipes. It's really easy. After one try, you'll be able to make it in your sleep. (But don't try this, please!)

Serve with a side salad, in a wrap or sandwich, or with a side of homemade Ketchup (page 265).

Serves 4

1½ cups **vegetable broth**

¼ cup **low-sodium tamari or soy sauce**

1 (14-ounce) block **extra-firm tofu**, pressed and cut into triangles (see page 34)

⅔ cup **cornstarch or tapioca flour**

¼ cup **nutritional yeast**

½ teaspoon **garlic powder**

½ teaspoon **finely ground black pepper**

1½ teaspoons **salt**, or to taste

Neutral cooking oil (see page 18), for pan-frying

In a small bowl, mix the vegetable broth and tamari. Transfer the mixture to a rimmed baking sheet or dish large enough to fit the tofu triangles in a single layer. Place the triangles in the broth mixture. Set aside for 3 minutes. Flip the tofu over and marinate the other sides for 3 more minutes.

In a small bowl, mix the cornstarch, nutritional yeast, garlic powder, black pepper, and salt. Transfer the cornstarch mixture to a small rimmed dish or baking sheet.

Preheat the oven to broil.

In a large nonstick skillet, heat enough oil to reach about halfway up the sides of the triangles over medium-high heat.

Remove the tofu from the broth mixture, allowing for any excess liquid to drip off. Coat the tofu in the cornstarch mixture, shaking off any excess. The tofu should have a dry outer layer of the cornstarch mixture.

When the oil starts to shimmer, add the tofu and cook for about 3 minutes on each side, or until golden brown. You may need to fry the tofu in batches so as not to overcrowd the skillet.

Transfer the tofu to a large baking sheet. Broil the triangles for about 2 minutes on each side, or until a crust forms. Serve immediately.

Crispy Baked Tofu Cubes

Follow this formula for perfectly crisp tofu every time. Enjoy your crispy tofu cubes as a topping for salads or pasta. Or add them to curries or soups for added texture and protein.

Serves 4

1 tablespoon **cornstarch**

¾ teaspoon **garlic powder**

¾ teaspoon **salt**, or to taste

¼ teaspoon **freshly ground black pepper**

1 (14-ounce) block **extra-firm tofu**, pressed and cut into ¾-inch cubes (see page 34)

1 tablespoon **olive oil** (optional)

Preheat the oven to 425°F. Line a large baking sheet with parchment paper or a silicone mat. Set aside.

In a small bowl, mix the cornstarch, garlic powder, salt, and pepper. Set aside.

Transfer the tofu cubes to a large plastic zip-top bag or reusable container. Add the olive oil (if using) and seal the bag. Gently toss the tofu to coat the cubes with the olive oil.

Add the cornstarch mixture to the bag and seal. Gently toss the tofu cubes until they are coated with the cornstarch.

Arrange the tofu cubes on the prepared baking sheet in an even single layer without touching. Bake for 15 minutes. Remove the cubes from the oven and flip them over. Bake for another 15 to 20 minutes, until crispy.

Cornflake-Crusted Tofu

1 (14-ounce) block **extra-firm tofu**, frozen and thawed (optional), pressed and cut into 12 rectangles (see page 34)

Paprika, for seasoning

Garlic powder, for seasoning

Finely ground black pepper, for seasoning

Salt, for seasoning

3 cups **cornflakes**, plus more as needed, crumbled (slightly larger than panko size)

½ cup **all-purpose flour**

Egg Replacer

½ cup **cornstarch**

2 teaspoons **paprika**

2 teaspoons **garlic powder**

1 teaspoon **finely ground black pepper**

½ teaspoon **salt**, or to taste

Olive oil nonstick cooking spray or neutral cooking oil (see page 18), for pan-frying

These crispy tofu rectangles far exceeded my expectations. You can always count on cornflakes! There's a rumor out there that cornflakes can help with PMS (premenstrual syndrome). I have struggled with PMS for the past five years (PMS is usually thought of as a teenage thing, but clearly, it's not), and when I read somewhere that the tryptophan in corn could help relieve my symptoms, I was more than happy to start indulging in cornflakes—the organic kind with no added sugars. In reality, I doubt that the tryptophan is really doing anything for my symptoms, but I tell my kids that it is, so they'll leave my box of cornflakes alone.

It turns out cornflakes have multiple uses, including in this delicious tofu. Pair these crispy rectangles with a side salad or roasted potatoes, or turn them into a wrap with chopped lettuce, red onions, avocado, and Aioli (page 254) or Ranch Dressing (page 259). They can also be enjoyed with a simple side of homemade Ketchup (page 265).

There are two awesome plant-based cooking techniques in this recipe that are worth keeping in your culinary toolbox.

- For a chewy, chicken-like texture, freeze the tofu in its packaging for at least 24 hours and then thaw in the refrigerator before pressing. It's even more yummy this way, but it does require planning ahead.

- A simple vegan egg replacer can be made by combining cornstarch, water, and seasonings in the ratio on page 216. (The texture should resemble beaten eggs.)

There are two options on page 216 for cooking your crusted tofu. Using an oil cooking spray makes things easier, but you can also pan-fry them.

Serves 3 (makes 12 rectangles)

Preheat the oven to 425°F, if using cooking method 1 (baking).

Sprinkle each tofu rectangle with a generous amount of paprika, garlic powder, black pepper, and salt. Rub the seasonings on the tofu. Set aside.

Transfer the cornflake crumbles into a large rimmed dish or plate. Transfer the flour to a separate plate.

Recipe continues

Make the egg replacer: In a medium bowl, stir the cornstarch, paprika, garlic powder, black pepper, salt, and ¾ cup water until fully incorporated. Transfer the mixture to a small rimmed dish or plate.

Coat each seasoned tofu rectangle with the egg replacer, flour, egg replacer (again), and cornflake crumbles—in that order. Spread the coated rectangles on a large nonstick baking sheet in a single layer.

Cooking method 1 *(bake):* Spray the rectangles with the cooking spray until they are evenly coated on both sides. Bake for 10 to 12 minutes, until golden brown on top. Flip them over and bake for 5 to 10 minutes more, until they are crispy and golden brown on both sides.

Cooking method 2 *(pan-fry):* In a large nonstick skillet, heat enough oil to reach about halfway up the sides of the rectangles over medium-high heat. Once the oil is hot, add the tofu and cook for about 3 minutes on each side, or until golden brown. You may need to fry in batches so as not to overcrowd the skillet.

Crispy Tofu Cutlets

½ cup **all-purpose flour**

1 tablespoon plus 1 teaspoon
   cornstarch or arrowroot

Salt

1 teaspoon **baking powder**

1 teaspoon **paprika**

1 teaspoon **onion powder**

1 teaspoon **garlic powder**

1 teaspoon **hot sauce**

1 (14-ounce) block **extra-firm tofu**,
   placed in the freezer for at least
   24 hours, thawed, and pressed
   (see page 34)

Coarsely ground black pepper

1 cup **panko bread crumbs**

Neutral cooking oil (see page 18),
   for pan-frying (optional)

Crispy on the outside and the good kind of chewy on the inside make these cutlets highly addictive. Freezing your tofu beforehand is a game changer. It transforms the tofu structurally, drawing out the moisture, and giving it a spongey texture that feels just like chicken. If you're short on time, you can skip this step. The recipe works just as well, but your cutlets won't have that same meaty texture.

So, plan ahead for this recipe and freeze your tofu in its original packaging for at least 24 hours. Give yourself about a day to defrost the tofu in the refrigerator.

For serving, you can slice the cutlets into strips and use them in sandwiches or wraps; or serve them on a bed of Asian-Inspired Crunchy Salad with Sesame Ginger Dressing (page 196); or with a side of steamed rice, and Teriyaki Sauce (page 264).

Serves 3 (makes 3 cutlets)

Preheat the oven to 400°F. Line a baking sheet with parchment paper or a silicone mat. Set aside.

In a medium bowl, mix the flour, cornstarch, 1 teaspoon salt, the baking powder, paprika, onion powder, garlic powder, hot sauce, and ½ cup water until it forms a smooth batter. Set aside.

Slice the tofu horizontally into three equal cutlets (see page 35). Season both sides with salt and pepper.

Spread the panko on a rimmed baking sheet.

Dip one tofu cutlet into the batter, coating all sides. Shake to remove any excess. Press the tofu into the panko until all sides are covered and set it on the prepared baking sheet. Repeat for the other two cutlets.

Cooking method 1: Heat a thin layer of oil in a large nonstick skillet over medium-high heat. Once the oil is hot, sear the tofu for 3 to 5 minutes on both sides, until golden brown. Place the cutlets onto the prepared baking sheet and bake for 7 minutes, then flip them over. Bake for about another 7 minutes, or until crispy.

Cooking method 2 *(oil-free):* Bake the panko-coated cutlets for about 25 minutes, or until crispy on both sides, flipping them over after 15 minutes.

If desired, slice the tofu cutlets into ¾-inch strips, or about 6 strips for each cutlet.

Soy Curls

8 ounces soy curls

1½ tablespoons cornstarch

1½ teaspoons salt, or to taste

1½ tablespoons neutral cooking
    oil (see page 18)

Stir-fry sauce of your choice
    (see pages 261–264)

Soy curls are becoming quite popular now that they are being discovered by more people, and for good reason. They are an excellent source of plant protein and have a delicious meaty texture, very similar to chicken's. They are pretty much tasteless on their own, but they easily absorb the flavors of sauces and marinades. Mix them into one of the stir-fry sauces (see pages 261–264) and serve with noodles or rice or use them to make fried rice. They're also delicious in marinara sauce and served with pasta.

If you don't see them in your local supermarket or health food store, they're available on Amazon. I buy the Butler brand, made with only whole non-GMO soybeans that are free of additives or preservatives.

Serves 4

Soak the soy curls in a large bowl with enough warm water to cover by about 1½ inches for 10 minutes. (Do not soak for longer than 10 minutes or they will lose their texture.) Drain in a colander and transfer to a large bowl. Sprinkle with the cornstarch and salt. Use your hands to gently toss the soy curls until they are coated with the dry ingredients.

Heat the oil in a large nonstick skillet or wok over medium-high heat. Add the soy curls and sauté for 8 to 10 minutes, until they are golden brown and have a slightly crispy outer layer. (You may have to cook the soy curls in batches. If the skillet is too crowded, they will steam instead of browning.)

Add your choice of stir-fry sauce or marinara sauce to the skillet and cook until warmed through. Or use them in another recipe that has a sauce component.

Tempeh Nuggets

1 (8-ounce) package tempeh

⅓ cup all-purpose flour

¼ teaspoon onion powder

¼ teaspoon garlic powder

Generous pinch of salt, or to taste

⅓ cup unsweetened nondairy milk

1 teaspoon vegan Worcestershire sauce

1 cup panko bread crumbs, plus more as needed

Neutral cooking oil (see page 18), for pan-frying

You absolutely won't believe you're eating tempeh here. My kids had no clue! Coated with a delicious bread-crumb batter and lightly fried until perfectly crisp, these nuggets are divine. They're also high in fiber and plant-based protein. What's not to love?

Enjoy these nuggets in a wrap or add them to a salad for protein and a delicious crunch. Or pair them with one of the Potato Sides (pages 223–234) and Ketchup (page 265) for a near fast-food experience. They also make a protein-rich snack. Serve with ketchup (preferably homemade), Aioli (page 254), or Sweet & Spicy Dipping Sauce (page 260).

Simmering the tempeh prior to slicing is optional, but I highly recommend taking this extra step as it removes the slightly bitter flavor.

Serves 2 (makes 8 nuggets)

In a medium saucepan, bring enough water to cover the tempeh by about 2 inches to a boil. Add the block of tempeh, reduce the heat, and simmer for 3 minutes. Drain the tempeh and pat it dry. Set aside to cool.

Slice the tempeh into 8 equal-sized rectangles (see page 36).

In a medium bowl, mix the flour, onion powder, garlic powder, and salt. Pour the milk into the bowl gradually, stirring continuously, until a smooth batter forms. Add the Worcestershire and stir to incorporate.

Transfer the panko to a small rimmed baking sheet or serving dish.

Add enough oil to cover the base of a large nonstick skillet to a depth of about ¼ inch. Heat the oil over medium-high heat until shimmering. Dip the tempeh rectangles, one at a time, into the batter mixture, shaking to remove any excess, followed by the panko, until they are fully coated. Place the coated rectangles into the skillet and cook for about 3 minutes on each side, or until golden brown. You may need to fry the tempeh in batches so as not to overcrowd the skillet.

Tempeh Bacon

1 (8-ounce) package **tempeh**

¼ cup **low-sodium tamari or soy sauce**

2 tablespoons **maple syrup**

1 teaspoon **garlic powder**

½ teaspoon **smoked paprika**

Pinch of **finely ground black pepper**

1½ tablespoons **neutral cooking oil** (see page 18)

This recipe is a big part of why I have three tempeh-loving girls. It's an ideal plant-based substitute for the bacon in a BLT sandwich or the meat in fried rice, or as a protein side for any meal.

Tempeh is made from partially cooked soybeans that are fermented by a type of mold. I'm probably not doing the best job of marketing tempeh to you right now, but in this situation, mold is a good thing. It adds nutrients to the soybeans and makes them easier to digest, which means tempeh doesn't cause bloating or gas like other bean products might. (Here I am, back to the whole gas and constipation thing!) Aside from not making you fart, tempeh is also loaded with protein and fiber. It's actually a complete source of protein, meaning it has all the essential amino acids. Did I mention it's also a good source of iron?

This recipe calls for the optional step of simmering the tempeh prior to slicing. I highly recommend taking this extra step as it removes the slightly bitter flavor. It also softens the tempeh, allowing it to absorb more of the marinade.

Serves 3

In a medium saucepan, bring enough water to cover the tempeh by about 2 inches to a boil. Add the block of tempeh, reduce the heat, and simmer for 3 minutes. Drain the tempeh and pat it dry. Set aside to cool.

Meanwhile, prepare the sauce by mixing the tamari, maple syrup, garlic powder, smoked paprika, and black pepper in a small bowl.

Slice the cooled tempeh into 8 to 12 equal-sized rectangles (see page 36). The thinner the rectangles, the crispier the bacon.

Heat the oil in a large skillet over medium-high heat. Once the oil starts to shimmer, place the tempeh into the skillet in a single layer and cook for about 3 minutes on each side, or until browned.

Add 1 tablespoon water to the skillet. Add the sauce and swirl the skillet to spread the sauce evenly over the tempeh. Flip the rectangles so both sides get coated in the sauce. Cook each side for 2 to 3 minutes, until there is no more sauce remaining and both sides are browned.

Chickpea Croutons

1 (15-ounce) can **chickpeas**, drained and rinsed, or 1½ cups cooked chickpeas

1 teaspoon **smoked paprika**

½ teaspoon **garlic powder**

¼ teaspoon **cayenne pepper**

1 tablespoon **olive oil**

1½ tablespoons **freshly squeezed lemon juice**, or to taste

Salt to taste

Use these culinary gems to add a crunch to soups and salads, as a stand-alone snack, as a topping for avocado toast, or to provide plant-based protein to any meal. The versatility of Chickpea Croutons is greater than one could ever imagine.

Kids absolutely love these. I'm yet to meet one who doesn't, and with three kids, I've met my fair share!

Rubbing the chickpeas between paper towels removes the skins. This makes them even crispier after roasting. It's not a required step, so if you're short on time you can skip it. Just know it's a game-changer.

Serves 3

Preheat the oven to 400°F. Line a large rimmed baking sheet with parchment paper or a silicone mat. Set aside.

In two batches, rub the chickpeas between large paper towels to remove the skins and dry the chickpeas. Transfer them to a large bowl.

In a small bowl, mix the smoked paprika, garlic powder, and cayenne. Add the olive oil and the spice blend to the chickpeas and mix with a spoon to incorporate the ingredients. Use your hands to rub the chickpeas until they are evenly coated with the olive oil and spices.

Spread the chickpeas on the prepared baking sheet in a single layer. Roast for 15 minutes. Remove the sheet from the oven and toss the chickpeas so they cook evenly. Roast for about 10 minutes more, or until the chickpeas start to become crispy and golden brown. Change the oven setting to broil and cook for 2 to 3 minutes more, until browned and very crispy. Be careful not to let them burn.

Season with lemon juice and salt.

Tangy Potato Salad

1 (1½-pound) bag **baby yellow potatoes**, halved

Salt

½ medium **red onion**, diced small (about ½ cup)

"Tangy, Sweet & a Little Bit Cheesy" Dressing for Salads or Roasted Veggies (page 256)

3 **celery stalks**, finely chopped (about ½ cup)

Freshly ground black pepper to taste

1 tablespoon chopped **fresh dill**, for garnish

The goal for this recipe is to end up with potatoes that are just the right texture to absorb the dressing. We start off by parboiling the potatoes in cold water so that they cook evenly as the water heats up. If we plunged them straight into boiling water, the outsides would cook first, resulting in unevenly cooked potatoes.

The red onion is soaked in water to remove the sulfur compound that gives it that harsh "biting" quality. Soaking tones down the harshness quite a bit.

This dish can be served either warm or chilled. I usually find myself eating a portion as soon as it's ready, and then refrigerating the remainder and enjoying it as a cold salad the next day.

Serves 4 to 5

Place the potatoes into a medium saucepan with about 6 cups (1½ quarts) water, or enough to cover them by about 2 inches. Bring the water to a boil, then reduce the heat, salt the water generously, and gently boil the potatoes for about 15 minutes, or until they are fork-tender. Drain the potatoes and transfer them to a large bowl. If desired, you can peel off the skins at this point.

While the potatoes are cooking, add the diced onion to a small bowl with enough cold water to cover. Let sit for 10 minutes before draining.

Add the drained onions to the bowl with the potatoes, along with the dressing and celery. Gently toss until they are evenly coated. Season with salt and pepper. Garnish with dill.

Enjoy as a warm side salad, or for a cold salad, refrigerate the dressed potatoes for about 30 minutes, or until chilled.

Perfectly Crisp Roasted Baby Potatoes

Salt

½ teaspoon baking soda

15 baby yellow potatoes, unpeeled

2½ tablespoons olive oil

2 large garlic cloves, minced

1 tablespoon fresh thyme leaves

1 tablespoon chopped fresh rosemary

¼ teaspoon crushed red pepper (optional)

Freshly ground black pepper to taste

This recipe incorporates a few tricks I learned from hours of research on how to get crisp potatoes while keeping the insides moist and delicious. After much testing and tweaking and obsessing over potatoes for longer than I'd like to admit, I think I finally nailed it.

How do we get the crispiest potatoes? We turn their outsides into a bit of a "hot mess," which becomes super crispy in the oven. In order to create this desirable hot mess, we start our potatoes in boiling water, so the outsides cook before the insides. And to make doubly sure those outsides get messy, we add some baking soda to the cooking water. This turns the water alkaline, which further breaks down that outside layer of the potatoes. Next, we give them a good shake to roughen up that soft outer layer we've created. Finally, we coat the potatoes with oil and roast the heck out of them at a high temperature. Not that hard, right?

This method works for peeled potatoes, too. Though I often leave the skins on, as that's where a lot of the fiber is.

I like to call these "Mia-inspired potatoes." My niece Mia loves these potatoes so much that she even ate all my failed attempts. Don't get me wrong, those failed attempts were still delicious, they just weren't potato perfection, which is what we're going for here.

Serves 3

Preheat the oven to 450°F. (If you have a convection oven, set to convection and preheat to 400°F.)

Heat 4 cups (1 quart) water in a medium saucepan over high heat until the water comes to a boil. Add 1 tablespoon salt, the baking soda, and potatoes and boil for about 20 minutes, or until they are fork-tender.

Meanwhile, heat the olive oil in a small skillet over medium heat. Add the garlic, thyme, rosemary, and crushed red pepper (if using) and cook for 2 to 3 minutes, stirring constantly, until the garlic is golden. Be careful not to let the garlic burn.

Strain the oil through a fine-mesh strainer into a small bowl, reserving the garlic and herbs in a separate bowl.

Drain the potatoes and place them back into the hot

Recipe continues

Practically Vegan

saucepan for 30 seconds to remove excess moisture and give them a good shake to roughen up the outsides.

Transfer the potatoes to a medium bowl and add about two-thirds of the reserved infused olive oil. Toss the potatoes until they are evenly coated with the oil. Add more oil as needed, without making the potatoes too greasy.

Transfer the potatoes to a rimmed nonstick baking sheet and spread them out in an even single layer. Roast for 20 minutes. Remove the potatoes from the oven and shake the baking sheet to release them. Flip them over with a thin spatula and poke the skins with a fork. Roast for about 30 minutes more, or until crispy and browned all over. (Check for doneness every 7 to 10 minutes, shaking the pan to move them around.)

Transfer the cooked potatoes to a large bowl and add the reserved garlic and herbs. Toss to coat.

Season with salt and pepper.

Smashed Potatoes

6 medium **Yukon Gold potatoes**, washed, peeled, and halved lengthwise

Salt

4 tablespoons **vegan butter**

½ cup thinly sliced **green onions** (about 6 green onions, green parts only)

¼ cup **unsweetened nondairy milk**, preferably oat milk

1 teaspoon **garlic powder**

Ground white pepper

More potato-cooking tips, friends, but this time for the ultimate smashed potatoes. What are smashed potatoes anyway? They're mashed potatoes, but not quite.

For this recipe, add your potatoes to the saucepan at the same time as your water, before cranking up the heat, so they cook more evenly. Be careful not to overcook the potatoes. Once they're cooked, place them back into the hot saucepan after draining so they dry out a bit for better texture. Don't overwork your potatoes when mashing them, or they'll end up all gooey!

We're using white pepper to season the potatoes to avoid having black specks in our beautiful, creamy yellow potatoes. But feel free to switch to black pepper if aesthetics aren't a concern for you.

Serves 4

Place the potatoes in a medium saucepan with enough cold water to cover by about 2 inches. Bring the water to a gentle boil before adding 1 teaspoon salt. Cover the saucepan and cook the potatoes for about 20 minutes, or until a knife can be inserted into the middle of a potato with almost no resistance.

Drain the potatoes and place them back into the hot saucepan for 1 minute to remove excess moisture. Transfer to a large bowl and pass them through a ricer (my favorite method) or mash them with a potato masher.

Melt the butter in a small skillet over medium-low heat. Add the green onions and cook for 1 to 2 minutes, until they start to become tender. Add the nondairy milk and cook until warmed through. Transfer the milk mixture to the bowl with the potatoes. Add the garlic powder and ¼ teaspoon white pepper. Stir to combine. Season with more salt and white pepper if necessary.

Crispy Top Potato Rounds

3 medium **russet potatoes**, peeled and sliced into ½-inch-thick rounds

4 tablespoons **vegan butter**

¾ teaspoon **dried thyme**

½ teaspoon **dried rosemary**

¼ teaspoon **finely ground black pepper**

3 **garlic cloves**, minced

½ cup **vegetable broth**

Salt to taste

These chubby, crispy top potatoes are always the first thing eaten on the table. The combination of the crispy top with the garlicky-flavored melt-in-your-mouth center makes them irresistible.

To avoid ending up with "Mushy Top Potato Rounds," the potatoes are soaked prior to roasting to remove the excess starch. They are then salted once they are out of the oven, so they remain crispy.

Serves 3

Preheat the oven to 425°F.

Place the potato rounds into a medium bowl with enough cold water to cover. Soak for 30 minutes. Drain the potatoes and dry them thoroughly with a kitchen towel or paper towel.

In a small skillet, melt the butter over low heat. Stir in the thyme, rosemary, and black pepper. Remove from the heat.

Transfer the potato rounds to a large rimmed baking sheet. Pour the melted herb butter over the potatoes. Use your hands to gently rub both sides of the potato rounds with the butter until they are evenly coated. Place the potatoes in a single layer.

Roast the potatoes for 15 minutes. Flip them over and roast for another 10 minutes. Meanwhile, mix the garlic into the vegetable broth. Remove the potato slices from the oven and flip one more time. Pour the broth onto the baking sheet without splashing any onto the tops of the potatoes. Gently move the sheet around until the broth is evenly distributed. Roast for about 10 minutes more, or until the potatoes are fork-tender and the tops are crispy. Remove from the oven and season with salt.

Deliciously Dressed Roasted Potatoes

3 small **russet potatoes**, peeled and cut into ½-inch cubes (about 2 cups)

1 tablespoon plus 1 teaspoon **olive oil**

¾ teaspoon **garlic powder**

Salt

½ medium **red onion**, diced (about ½ cup)

3 **garlic cloves**, minced

¼ teaspoon **paprika**

⅛ teaspoon **cayenne pepper**

2 tablespoons **vegan mayonnaise**

1½ teaspoons **apple cider vinegar**

1½ teaspoons **Dijon mustard**

½ teaspoon **sriracha**

1 tablespoon chopped **fresh parsley**, for garnish

These potatoes are the "once you pop, you can't stop" variety. There are a few steps involved in creating maybe the best potatoes you'll ever have, seasoned from start to finish and then topped with a generous drizzle of mayo-mustard dressing with a sriracha kick.

We're going to soak the potatoes in water before roasting them. This removes some of the starch so they cook more evenly and become even crispier.

Serves 2

Place the potatoes into a medium bowl with enough cold water to cover. Soak the potatoes for 30 minutes.

Preheat the oven to 450°F. Line a large baking sheet with parchment paper or a silicone mat.

Drain the potatoes and dry them thoroughly with a kitchen towel or paper towel. Transfer the potatoes to a medium bowl. Add 1 tablespoon of the olive oil, the garlic powder, and a dash of salt. Use your hands to rub the potatoes until they are evenly coated with the oil and seasonings.

Spread the potatoes on the prepared baking sheet in an even single layer and roast for 20 minutes. Toss the potatoes and roast for another 15 to 20 minutes, tossing them every 10 minutes, until the potatoes are fork-tender and golden brown. Sprinkle with salt and set aside to cool.

Meanwhile, heat the remaining 1 teaspoon olive oil in a medium skillet over medium heat. Add the red onion and cook for about 7 minutes, or until they brown slightly. Add the garlic, paprika, cayenne, and a pinch of salt. Cook for 1 minute more. Transfer to a large bowl. Add the potatoes and gently toss until the potatoes are coated in the onion mixture. Set aside.

In a small bowl, mix the mayonnaise, cider vinegar, mustard, and sriracha to blend.

Drizzle the dressing over the potatoes and gently toss. Season with salt and garnish with parsley.

Roasted Sweet Potato Chunks

The deep orange color of sweet potatoes comes from beta-carotene, which your body converts to vitamin A. So yes, sweet potatoes really are good for your eyes. They're also high in fiber, keeping us regular and helping us not to overeat.

How do we get those roasted sweet potato chunks to melt in your mouth and be packed with flavor? We season the heck out of them before roasting.

Serves 2

1 large **sweet potato**, peeled and cut into 1-inch pieces (about 3 cups)

1 teaspoon **dried oregano**

½ teaspoon **garlic powder**

½ teaspoon **paprika**

¼ teaspoon **salt**, or to taste

2 tablespoons **olive oil**

1 tablespoon chopped **cilantro**, for garnish

Preheat the oven to 425°F. Line a large baking sheet with parchment paper or a silicone mat.

Place the sweet potato chunks in a medium bowl.

In a small bowl, mix the oregano, garlic powder, paprika, and salt. Add the seasonings and olive oil to the sweet potato chunks. Use your hands to rub the seasonings and olive oil on the chunks until they are evenly coated.

Spread the sweet potato pieces on the prepared baking sheet in an even single layer. Roast for 15 minutes. Remove from the oven and toss. Roast for about another 12 minutes, or until the chunks are tender and charred around the edges.

Garnish with cilantro and serve.

Baked Sweet Potato

2 medium **sweet potatoes,** scrubbed clean

Salt and freshly ground black pepper to taste

I'm often asked on social media how I bake my sweet potatoes. My method is very simple, maybe too simple to include in a cookbook. But I'm including it anyway because, for some of you, this simple gem of a recipe may change your relationship with sweet potatoes forever.

For serving, I like to slice my sweet potatoes lengthwise and load them with beans, chili, BBQ Chickpeas (page 80), or Chickpea Croutons (page 222), topped with a dollop of Easy Guacamole (page 252). And when I really feel like splurging, I add Sour Cream (page 249). Baked sweet potatoes are also delicious with tahini or nut butter.

Alternatively, you can scoop out the flesh and use it to make sweet potato soup or to sweeten and thicken a sauce or curry. And if all you're craving is a comforting side, slice and top it with a generous pat of vegan butter. I could honestly go on forever about the culinary uses of the humble sweet potato.

Serves 2 with a filling of your choice

Preheat the oven to 425°F. Line a small baking sheet with parchment paper for easy cleanup (this is optional).

Pierce the sweet potatoes all over with a fork.

Transfer the potatoes to the baking sheet. Bake for 20 minutes before flipping them over. Continue baking for about 25 minutes more, or until they are easily pierced with a fork in the thickest part.

Set aside to cool before slicing them in half lengthwise. Be careful not to slice all the way through the bottom, as you want the halves to stay attached. Season with salt and pepper.

Coconut-Infused Sweet Potato Rounds

These pan-fried sweet potato rounds have a delicious coconut crust that's mouthwatering. What could be better than a coconut crust? A *crispy* coconut crust, that's what! Inspired by my love for creamy coconut curries with sweet potato, this flavor combo is seriously addictive. Serve with Sweet & Spicy Dipping Sauce (page 260) for even more yumminess.

For this recipe, it's best to use a wide round sweet potato so you get large round slices. And make sure to stir the coconut milk before using as it tends to separate in the can, and this recipe doesn't use the entire can.

Serves 3

¾ cup **all-purpose flour**

1 teaspoon **garlic powder**

¾ teaspoon **paprika**

½ teaspoon **finely ground black pepper**

½ teaspoon **salt**

Batter

½ cup **cornstarch**

2 teaspoons **paprika**

2 teaspoons **garlic powder**

1 teaspoon **finely ground black pepper**

½ teaspoon **salt**, or to taste

¾ cup canned **unsweetened coconut milk**

Neutral cooking oil (see page 18), for pan-frying

1 medium-large **sweet potato**, peeled and sliced into ½-inch-thick rounds (about 7 pieces)

Preheat the oven to 400°F.

Line a large baking sheet with parchment paper or a silicone mat.

In a medium bowl, mix the flour, garlic powder, paprika, black pepper, and salt. Transfer the flour mixture to a medium rimmed dish or tray.

Make the batter: Combine the cornstarch, paprika, garlic powder, black pepper, and salt in a medium bowl and mix well until the spices are fully incorporated into the cornstarch. Add the coconut milk and stir until no lumps remain.

In a large nonstick skillet, heat enough oil to reach about a third of the way up the sides of the sweet potato rounds over medium-high heat. Once the oil is shimmering, coat one sweet potato round with the batter, then with the flour, and then with the batter once more, shaking each time to remove any excess flour or batter. Place it in the hot oil and repeat for each sweet potato round. Cook for about 4 minutes on each side, or until dark golden brown. (You may need to fry the sweet potato in batches, so as not to overcrowd the skillet.) Place the rounds onto a paper-towel-lined plate to remove any excess oil.

Transfer the rounds to the prepared baking sheet. Bake for 5 minutes before flipping them over, then bake for about 3 minutes more, or until they are just fork-tender. Serve immediately.

Garlicky Rice

This rice dish pairs well with beans, curries, chilis, stir-fries, and almost anything your heart desires. You can use any variety of rice you like for this recipe. Whenever I eat this dish, I think of my foodie-friend Catherine, who always says, "Rice is life!"

Previously refrigerated rice is best for this recipe, but freshly cooked rice works, too.

Makes 1 cup

1½ tablespoons **sesame oil**

½ medium **yellow onion**, diced (about 1 cup)

3 **garlic cloves**, minced

1 cup **refrigerated leftover rice**

Low-sodium tamari or soy sauce, or coconut aminos to taste

Salt to taste

Heat the sesame oil in a medium nonstick skillet over medium-high heat. Add the onion and garlic and cook for about 3 minutes, or until the onion is translucent.

Add the rice and mix to incorporate the garlic and onion. Cook for about 3 minutes, or until the rice is heated through. Add tamari and salt to taste.

Coconut Quinoa

Quinoa is classified as a whole grain but it's technically an edible seed. It's also a complete protein and a good source of fiber, but starch is its main component, so you've found it with the potato and starchy sides. That being said, all that you really need to know is that it's incredibly healthy and I eat a lot of it. Do you know that there are more than 120 known varieties of quinoa?

Serves 3

1 cup **white quinoa**

1 (14-ounce) can **unsweetened coconut milk**

¼ teaspoon **salt**

Rinse the quinoa in a fine-mesh strainer. Transfer to a medium saucepan and toast over medium heat for about 3 minutes, or until light golden brown, stirring constantly.

Add the coconut milk, ½ cup water, and the salt. Stir to combine. Bring to a boil, then reduce the heat to a gentle simmer. Cover and cook for 15 minutes. Remove from the heat and set aside to steam for 5 minutes before removing the lid. Fluff with a fork.

Lemony Cauliflower Rice

3 tablespoons **olive oil**

1 medium **yellow onion**, diced (1¾ cups)

1 (12-ounce) package **frozen riced cauliflower**, thawed and drained (3½ cups)

⅓ cup chopped **fresh cilantro**

1½ tablespoons **freshly squeezed lemon juice**, plus more to taste

Salt to taste

This is not a starchy side in actuality, but it tends to be eaten as one, which is why I included it in this section. It's a low-starch alternative to rice when you're in the mood for something lighter, or if you're trying to increase your daily veggie intake. It's loaded with all the same nutrients as cauliflower—obviously—including fiber, vitamin C, and potassium. One of the best things about a high-fiber diet is that you're much less likely to overeat, because that fiber really fills you up. I'm not an advocate of dieting, but I always joke that if someone really wants to lose weight, they should go on the cauliflower diet! Just a few large florets, and you're stuffed.

Serves 4

Heat the olive oil in a large skillet over medium-high heat. Add the onion and cook for about 7 minutes, or until golden brown at the edges.

Add the cauliflower and cook for 3 minutes more, stirring frequently. Remove from the heat.

Stir in the cilantro and lemon juice. Season with salt and adjust the lemon juice to taste.

Spicy Peanut Miso Noodles

6 ounces **udon or rice noodles**

Spicy Peanut Miso Sauce

1½ tablespoons **dark soy sauce or soy sauce**

1 tablespoon **low-sodium tamari or soy sauce**

1 tablespoon plus 1½ teaspoons **maple syrup**

1 tablespoon **mellow (white) miso**

1 tablespoon **smooth peanut, almond, or cashew butter**

1 teaspoon **sesame oil**

½ teaspoon **chili-garlic sauce**

These saucy noodles will 100 percent satisfy your noodle cravings, and they will do so in less than 10 minutes! Plus, they have healthy fats and protein from the nut butter and all the goodness of miso.

They are delicious on their own or paired with Tempeh Bacon (page 221), Crispy Baked Tofu Cubes (page 213), Tempeh Nuggets (page 219) or one of the Asian Fake-Out recipes (pages 143–161).

This sauce is not just for noodles. It's also great in stir-fries (vegetable, tofu, tempeh, chickpea, or soy curls). It's rich in umami, slightly sweet and spicy, and has a delectable nutty flavor.

Serves 3

Cook the noodles according to the package directions. Drain and set aside.

Make the spicy peanut miso sauce: In a medium bowl, mix the dark soy sauce, tamari, maple syrup, miso, peanut butter, sesame oil, chili-garlic sauce, and 1 tablespoon water. Stir to make sure the miso is fully dissolved before using.

Heat the sauce in a medium saucepan over medium-low heat for about 3 minutes, or until it is warmed through and starts to thicken. Remove the saucepan from the heat and stir in the noodles until they are fully coated with the sauce.

Cheesy Savory Pancakes

2 tablespoons **flax meal** (ground flaxseeds)

1½ cups **unsweetened nondairy milk**

1 tablespoon **apple cider vinegar**

1½ cups **whole-wheat pastry flour or all-purpose flour**

½ cup **cornmeal** (medium or fine grind)

1½ teaspoons **baking powder**

½ teaspoon **baking soda**

1 teaspoon **garlic powder**

1 teaspoon **onion powder**

1 teaspoon **salt**, or to taste

2 tablespoons **neutral cooking oil** (see page 18), plus more for cooking

1 cup shredded **nondairy cheese**

I came up with this savory pancake recipe when reminiscing about the tempeh chili I had eaten the night before. I wanted something new and exciting to pair with my chili. These pancakes turned out to be a tasty accompaniment. When testing this recipe, I discovered they were also delicious on their own. The first batch never made it to the chili.

They're super fun to make. The recipe uses two essential vegan baking substitutes—vegan buttermilk and "flax eggs."

For a change, we are not using nutritional yeast for the cheesy flavor but store-bought vegan shredded cheese. I felt like splurging a bit on this one, and it was well worth it. The pancakes turned out amazing.

I prefer using medium-grind cornmeal in this recipe for more texture. Fine grind will also work, but your pancakes will be slightly denser.

Serves 4 (makes 16 pancakes)

Mix the flax meal with 5 tablespoons warm water in a small bowl to make the "flax eggs." Set aside for at least 10 minutes to gel.

Mix together the nondairy milk and cider vinegar in a medium bowl. Set aside for 10 minutes. This will curdle to make vegan buttermilk.

Whisk together the flour, cornmeal, baking powder, baking soda, garlic powder, onion powder, and salt in a large mixing bowl. Add the flax eggs, vegan buttermilk, and oil to the bowl and mix until just combined. Do not overmix.

Fold in the cheese.

In a large nonstick skillet, heat a drizzle of oil over medium heat. Using ¼ cup for each pancake, pour the batter, forming a rough circle, and cook for about 2 minutes, or until bubbles start appearing on top. Make as many pancakes at once as will fit, being sure to leave room to flip them. Flip the pancakes and cook on the other side for about 2 minutes more, or until golden brown. Drizzle more oil into the skillet between cooking each batch of pancakes. Serve immediately.

Sesame Garlic Ramen Noodles

Sauce

1 tablespoon **dark soy sauce or soy sauce**

1 tablespoon **low-sodium tamari or soy sauce**

1½ teaspoons **maple syrup**

1 teaspoon **rice vinegar**

1 teaspoon **toasted sesame oil**

1 teaspoon **chili-garlic sauce**

½ teaspoon **gochujang (Korean chili sauce) or sriracha**

2 packages **ramen noodles** (about 2.5 ounces each)

1 tablespoon **sesame oil**

4 small **garlic cloves**, minced

2 **green onions**, sliced (green and light green parts only)

2 teaspoons **toasted sesame seeds** (see page 40), for garnish

I've yet to meet someone who does not like ramen. Let me rephrase that. I've yet to meet someone who does not *love* ramen.

These noodles are so flavorful that they don't really need a companion. I can eat a whole bowl of just these ramen noodles. But they're also yummy with Cornflake-Crusted Tofu (page 214), Tempeh Nuggets (page 219), Tempeh Bacon (page 221), Crispy Baked Tofu Cubes (page 213), and any of the Asian Fake-Out recipes (pages 143–161).

If you're using ramen noodles that come in a soup package, save the soup base (seasoning) pouch for other uses. Don't add it to this recipe.

Serves 2

Make the sauce: In a small bowl, mix the dark soy sauce, tamari, maple syrup, rice vinegar, toasted sesame oil, chili-garlic sauce, and gochujang. Set aside.

In a small saucepan, bring enough water to cover the ramen noodles by about 2 inches to a boil. Once the water is boiling, add the noodles and cook for 1 minute. Reduce the heat to a gentle boil and cook for about 3 minutes more, or until the noodles just soften. While the noodles are cooking, gently separate them using a fork. Strain and rinse with cold water. Set aside.

Heat the sesame oil in a large skillet over medium-high heat. Sauté the garlic and green onions for 1 minute, until fragrant. Add the ramen noodles and sauce and cook for about 2 minutes more, or until the sauce has thickened and the noodles are fully coated and warmed through. Stir constantly.

Garnish with toasted sesame seeds.

Pita Chips

¼ cup **olive oil**

¼ teaspoon **garlic powder**

¼ teaspoon **black pepper**

½ teaspoon **dried oregano**

2 large **pita rounds** (about 8 inches), each cut into 8 equal-size triangles

Salt to taste

These delightful, toasty chips are made for dipping into Light & Fluffy Hummus (page 251), Easy Guacamole (page 252), or Tzatziki (page 255). One of my favorite combos is the Mediterranean-Inspired Salad (page 192) with these chips and Light & Fluffy Hummus. It combines three sides to make one complete meal.

Serves 3

Preheat the oven to 400°F.

In a small bowl, mix together the olive oil, garlic powder, pepper, and oregano.

Spread the pita triangles out on a large baking sheet in a single layer. Use a pastry brush to apply the seasoned oil generously to both sides of the triangles.

Bake for 5 minutes. Remove from the oven and flip the triangles over. Bake for about 5 minutes more, or until golden brown and crispy.

Sprinkle the triangles with salt immediately after removing them from the oven.

Cornbread Mug Cake

1½ teaspoons olive oil

3 tablespoons cornmeal

2 tablespoons oat or all-purpose flour

¼ teaspoon baking powder

Pinch of salt

3 tablespoons unsweetened nondairy milk

2 teaspoons maple syrup

Mug cakes are exactly that: a cake inside a mug. No oven required. This recipe takes just a few minutes to prepare, and the microwave cook time is 1½ minutes. There's something really comforting about eating cake out of your favorite mug.

The recipe makes enough for one mug cake. But it's easy to make as many as you'd like. Just repeat the recipe and use a different mug. But don't microwave more than one at the same time as this will change the cooking time.

Enjoy this mug cake with with many of the recipes in chapter 2 (Beans & Chili, pages 73-92) and possibly a side of Easy Guacamole (page 252).

Serves 1

Grease an 8- to 10-ounce microwave-safe mug with ½ teaspoon of the olive oil.

Mix the cornmeal, oat flour, baking powder, salt, nondairy milk, maple syrup, and the remaining 1 teaspoon olive oil in a measuring cup or pitcher.

Pour the batter into the greased mug. Microwave for 1½ minutes. Carefully remove from the microwave and enjoy.

Chapter 8

Dips, Dressings & Sauces

Adding a dip, dressing, or sauce are all ways to make dishes more palatable and exciting. They can also add nutritional value. Take a sheet pan of roasted veggies, for example. Sure, they're delicious on their own, but now imagine adding a slather of Tahini Dijon Dressing (page 260). In my experience, kids (and even grown-ups) will devour them in no time at all. Plus, the dressing adds heart-healthy fats that help the body absorb valuable nutrients more readily. I like to say, "Just a spoonful of fat helps the vegetables go down . . . in the most delightful way!"

There's a wide selection of dressings and sauces in this chapter. Mix and match what you serve them with, and don't be afraid to try something new. There are also some suggestions for how to use them.

Adjust the quantities of these recipes as needed while maintaining the same ratio of ingredients.

Sour Cream

1 cup **raw cashews**, soaked, drained, and rinsed (see page 39)

1 tablespoon **freshly squeezed lemon juice**

1 tablespoon **apple cider vinegar**

1 tablespoon **nutritional yeast**

½ teaspoon **garlic powder**

½ teaspoon **onion powder**

½ teaspoon **salt**

1 tablespoon chopped **fresh chives**

Use this as you would traditional sour cream. Serve It with many of the recipes in chapter 2 (Beans & Chili, pages 73–92) and chapter 4 (Burgers & Patties, Stuff It, Wrap It, Top It, pages 113–138), or use it to brighten soups and make them extra creamy. There are so many uses for this tangy and velvety dip.

Makes about ⅔ cup

Place the cashews in a high-speed blender. Add ⅓ cup water, the lemon juice, cider vinegar, nutritional yeast, garlic powder, onion powder, and salt. Blend on high until smooth. Garnish with chives.

Refrigerate any remaining dip in an airtight container for up to 3 days.

Pita Chips, page 243

Light & Fluffy Hummus

1 (15-ounce) can **chickpeas**, drained and rinsed, or 1½ cups cooked chickpeas

1½ teaspoons **baking soda**

1 medium-large **garlic clove**, minced

2½ tablespoons **freshly squeezed lemon juice** (about 1 large lemon)

Zest of ½ **lemon**

2 tablespoons **tahini**

½ teaspoon **salt**, or to taste

Serving (Optional)

Drizzle of **extra-virgin olive oil**

Dash of **paprika**

Chopped **fresh parsley**

There are a few hacks to making really good hummus passed down from renowned chefs, and this recipe takes full advantage of them. This hummus is so good, I was tempted to write that it only serves one because it was so hard for me to stop taste testing this creamy, lemony, and garlicky dip.

The first hack is to soak the chickpeas in hot water with baking soda. Baking soda softens the chickpeas. It also makes their skins fall off more easily. The longer you soak them, the creamier your hummus, but even a short soak makes a significant difference.

Hack number two is to rub the chickpeas between two dish towels to remove the skins. This step is not essential as the skins are softened from the baking soda. But it makes enough of a difference that if you have the time, it's worth doing. If you're short on time, go ahead and skip this step. Your hummus will still be scrumptious and creamy.

The final hack I'm aware of is to add ice cubes to the food processor while blending your hummus. This gives it the most incredible, light and fluffy consistency that store-bought hummus lacks. Are you sold yet? Let's go make some hummus.

Serves 5 (makes about 2 cups)

Transfer the chickpeas to a medium bowl. Add boiling water to cover by about 2 inches. Mix in the baking soda. Set aside for at least 10 minutes.

Drain and rinse the chickpeas. Place them between two dish towels and rub back and forth to remove the skins. (You may need to do this in batches.)

Transfer the chickpeas to a food processor with the garlic. Process for about 1 minute, or until the chickpeas are a powder-like consistency.

Add the lemon juice, lemon zest, tahini, and salt. While the hummus is blending, add 3 ice cubes through the feed tube. Process for about 4 minutes, or until very creamy. (Scrape the sides and base of the bowl as needed.)

Drizzle with olive oil, and garnish with paprika and parsley for serving, if desired.

Easy Guacamole

1 large avocado, roughly mashed

2 small plum tomatoes, diced small (⅔ cup)

½ small red onion, finely diced (¼ cup)

½ small jalapeño, seeded and minced

1 teaspoon freshly squeezed lime juice, plus more to taste

¼ teaspoon salt, or to taste

1 small garlic clove

Did you know that avocados are actually a type of berry? These creamy, delicious "berries" are an easy way to add healthy fats to a meal, and they're an excellent source of fiber, potassium, and magnesium. Magnesium and potassium can help relieve muscle cramps by loosening tight muscles, making avocados a great pre- and post-workout snack. All the more reason to indulge in avocado toast after your morning run!

This guacamole pairs well with Pita Chips (page 243) and most of the recipes in chapter 2 (Beans & Chili, pages 73–92) and chapter 4 (Burgers & Patties, Stuff It, Wrap It, Top It, pages 113–138).

Serves 2 (makes about 1 cup)

In a medium bowl, mix the avocado, tomatoes, red onion, jalapeño, lime juice, and salt. Grate the garlic using a Microplane or fine grater directly into the bowl and stir to incorporate. Adjust the lime juice to taste. Eat immediately, as guacamole doesn't keep very well.

Cashew Cream

1 cup **raw cashews**, soaked, drained, and rinsed (see page 39)

½ teaspoon **salt**

Cashew cream is the gold standard in vegan substitutes for dairy-based creams. Use it to thicken sauces or soups, or to make them creamier, or as a base for making salad dressings or dips. Depending on its intended use, you can add different herbs, spices, or condiments to this recipe, such as oregano, thyme, paprika, garlic powder or cloves, onion powder, olive oil, or lemon juice. You can even add some nutritional yeast for a cheesy flavor. One of my favorite ways to use cashew cream is to add garlic powder and nutritional yeast and stir it into my pasta sauce for an extra cheesy and creamy taste.

Start with a cashew-to-water ratio of 2:1, and then adjust the amount of water as needed to reach the desired consistency, depending on its use.

It's best to use a high-speed blender to make nut creams, as they turn out much smoother. Remember to soak the cashews either overnight or in very hot water for at least 1 hour before blending. If your high-speed blender is very powerful, you may not need to soak them at all.

Makes about ½ cup

Place the cashews, ½ cup water, and the salt in a high-speed blender. Blend on high until smooth, adding more water as needed, until the cream is the desired consistency.

Refrigerate any remaining cashew cream in an airtight container for up to 3 days.

Aioli

1 small **lemon**

2 **garlic cloves**

½ cup **vegan mayonnaise**

Salt to taste

Lemony, garlicky, creamy, and oh-so dreamy. I love aioli.

Enjoy your aioli with many of the recipes in chapter 4 (Burgers & Patties, Stuff It, Wrap It, Top It, pages 113–138).

Makes about ½ cup

Grate the zest of the lemon and the garlic using a Microplane or fine grater into a small bowl. Stir in the mayonnaise and 1 teaspoon lemon juice and combine well. Season with salt.

Refrigerate any remaining aioli in an airtight container for up to 3 days.

Practically Vegan

Tzatziki

1 (5.3-ounce) container **cashew yogurt or coconut yogurt**

Juice of ½ **lemon**

½ tablespoon **white wine vinegar or rice vinegar**

1 tablespoon **olive oil**

1 small **garlic clove**

½ medium **cucumber**, peeled and grated

½ tablespoon chopped **fresh dill**

Salt and freshly ground black pepper to taste

Tzatziki is a refreshing sauce made with creamy yogurt, cucumbers, and fresh garlic. It's good for balancing spices and can be served with roasted veggies, Pita Chips (page 243), Sweet Potato Falafels (page 130), and several of the recipes in chapter 4 (Burgers & Patties, Stuff It, Wrap It, Top It, pages 113–138). I also like using it as a salad dressing.

Makes about ¾ cup

In a medium bowl, combine the yogurt, lemon juice, vinegar, and olive oil and blend well. Grate the garlic using a Microplane or fine grater directly into the bowl and stir to incorporate. Mix in the cucumber and dill. Season with salt and pepper.

Refrigerate any remaining sauce in an airtight container for up to 2 days.

Yogurt Drizzle Sauce

1 cup **unsweetened plant-based yogurt**

Zest of 1 **lemon**

1 tablespoon **freshly squeezed lemon juice**

1 tablespoon chopped **fresh cilantro**

2 teaspoons chopped **fresh parsley**

½ teaspoon **ground cumin**

Salt to taste

Fresh parsley and cilantro make this an ideal sauce for brightening dishes and adding an abundance of nutrients found in fresh herbs.

Drizzle it over salads, buddha bowls, roasted veggies, or Chickpea Croutons (page 222). This sauce also pairs well with many of the recipes in chapter 3 (Curry, pages 97–109) and chapter 4 (Burgers & Patties, Stuff It, Wrap It, Top It, pages 113–138).

Makes about 1 cup

In a small bowl, mix together the yogurt, lemon zest and juice, cilantro, parsley, and cumin until well blended. Season with salt.

Refrigerate any remaining sauce in an airtight container for up to 2 days.

"Tangy, Sweet & a Little Bit Cheesy" Dressing for Salads or Roasted Veggies

No blending required. This versatile dressing pairs well with salads, potatoes, chickpeas, and roasted veggies. Plus, it packs in those essential B vitamins from the nutritional yeast.

Makes about ¾ cup

In a medium bowl, mix the mayonnaise, mustard, lemon juice, tamari, olive oil, cider vinegar, nutritional yeast, and garlic. Add the maple syrup to taste and blend well.

Refrigerate any remaining dressing in an airtight container for up to 3 days.

½ cup **vegan mayonnaise**

1 tablespoon **Dijon mustard**

2 tablespoons **freshly squeezed lemon juice**

1 tablespoon **low-sodium tamari or soy sauce**

1 tablespoon **extra-virgin olive oil**

1½ teaspoons **apple cider vinegar**

2 tablespoons **nutritional yeast**

1 teaspoon minced **garlic**

1 to 2 teaspoons **maple syrup,** or to taste

Multipurpose Dressing or Dip

This creamy four-ingredient dressing has a spicy kick and is perfect for salads, roasted potatoes, oven fries, and roasted veggies.

Makes about ⅓ cup

¼ cup **vegan mayonnaise**

1 tablespoon **apple cider vinegar**

1 tablespoon **Dijon mustard**

1 teaspoon **sriracha**

In a small bowl, mix the mayonnaise, cider vinegar, mustard, and sriracha until blended.

Refrigerate any remaining dip in an airtight container for up to 3 days.

Sesame Ginger Salad Dressing

This Asian-inspired salad dressing has an addictive sesame flavor and a hint of sweetness. The addition of tahini also makes it a good source of heart-healthy fats.

Makes about ⅔ cup

½ cup **rice vinegar**

2½ tablespoons **tahini**

1½ tablespoons **Dijon or stone-ground mustard**

2 teaspoons **low-sodium tamari or soy sauce**

1 teaspoon **toasted sesame oil**

1 (½-inch) piece **fresh ginger**, finely grated or 2 teaspoons **ground ginger**

3 tablespoons **maple syrup**, or to taste

Salt to taste

In a small bowl, mix the rice vinegar, tahini, mustard, tamari, toasted sesame oil, ginger, and maple syrup. Whisk until smooth. Season with salt.

Refrigerate any remaining dressing in an airtight container for up to 3 days.

Vegan Caesar Salad Dressing

⅓ cup **raw cashews**, soaked, drained, and rinsed (see page 39)

3½ tablespoons **nutritional yeast**

1 **garlic clove**

½ teaspoon **dulse flakes or granules**

Zest of ½ **lemon**

2 tablespoons **freshly squeezed lemon juice**

2 teaspoons **Dijon mustard**

1 teaspoon **vegan Worcestershire sauce**

1 teaspoon **low-sodium tamari or soy sauce**

¼ teaspoon **maple syrup**

2 teaspoons **extra-virgin olive oil**

Salt and freshly ground black pepper to taste

Seaweed flakes and vegan Worcestershire sauce mimic the briny flavor of anchovies, a cornerstone of traditional Caesar salads. Nutritional yeast gives this dressing its cheesy flavor and adds essential B vitamins.

Makes about ⅓ cup

Place the cashews in a high-speed blender. Add the nutritional yeast, garlic, dulse flakes, lemon zest and juice, mustard, Worcestershire, tamari, maple syrup, olive oil, and 3 tablespoons water. Blend on high until smooth. Transfer the dressing to a small bowl. Season with salt and pepper.

Refrigerate any remaining dressing in an airtight container for up to 2 days.

Ranch Dressing

This is my daughter Nikita's all-time favorite dressing. She would add it to everything if she could!

I like to use it for drizzling over salads, buddha bowls, roasted veggies, or Chickpea Croutons (page 222). It's also delicious with many of the recipes from chapter 4 (Burgers & Patties, Stuff It, Wrap It, Top It, pages 113–138).

Makes about 1 cup

¼ cup **unsweetened nondairy milk**

¾ teaspoon **apple cider vinegar**

¾ cup **vegan mayonnaise**

1 large **garlic clove**, finely minced

¼ teaspoon **freshly squeezed lemon juice**

½ teaspoon **onion powder**

½ teaspoon **dried dill**

⅛ teaspoon **paprika**

⅛ teaspoon **ground mustard seed**

Pinch of **cayenne pepper**

2 tablespoons chopped **fresh parsley**

In a small bowl, mix the nondairy milk and cider vinegar to make vegan buttermilk. Set aside.

In a medium bowl, whisk the mayonnaise, garlic, lemon juice, onion powder, dill, paprika, ground mustard, and cayenne until well combined. Stir in the vegan buttermilk and chopped parsley.

Refrigerate any remaining dressing in an airtight container for up to 2 days.

Maple Dijon Dressing

This is a vegan version of traditional honey Dijon dressing for salads. It's light and creamy in texture and perfectly sweet and tangy in flavor.

Makes about ½ cup

¼ cup **Dijon mustard**

1 tablespoon plus 2 teaspoons **maple syrup**

2 tablespoons **vegan mayonnaise**

½ teaspoon **apple cider vinegar**

Pinch of **smoked paprika**

1 **garlic clove**

Salt to taste

In a medium bowl, mix the mustard, maple syrup, mayonnaise, cider vinegar, and smoked paprika until combined. Grate the garlic using a Microplane or a fine grater directly into the bowl and mix. Season with salt.

Refrigerate any remaining dressing in an airtight container for up to 3 days.

Tahini Dijon Dressing

This is similar to Maple Dijon Dressing (page 259), except that tahini replaces the mayonnaise for an extra dose of those healthy fats, and freshly squeezed lemon juice adds a fresh and tangy flavor. Drizzle on salads and roasted veggies.

Makes about 1½ cups

½ cup **Dijon mustard**

½ cup **tahini**

¼ cup **apple cider vinegar**

2 tablespoons **maple syrup**, or to taste

2 tablespoons **freshly squeezed lemon juice**

Salt and freshly ground black pepper to taste

In a medium bowl, whisk the mustard, tahini, cider vinegar, maple syrup, lemon juice, and ½ cup water until combined. Adjust the maple syrup to taste. Season with salt and pepper.

Refrigerate any remaining dressing in an airtight container for up to 5 days.

Sweet & Spicy Dipping Sauce

Sweet and spicy is a classic flavor combo for good reason. Chili oil and crushed red pepper add a fiery kick to this simple and versatile dipping sauce. Enjoy it with Tempeh Nuggets (page 219), Chickpea Fritters (page 129), Potato Tofu Patties (page 123), Crispy Tofu Cutlets (page 217), and Cornflake-Crusted Tofu (page 214).

Makes about ⅓ cup

3 tablespoons **rice vinegar**

2 tablespoons **low-sodium soy sauce or tamari**

1 teaspoon **chili oil**

½ teaspoon **sugar or maple syrup**

¼ teaspoon **crushed red pepper**

In a small bowl, whisk the rice vinegar, soy sauce, chili oil, sugar, and crushed red pepper until smooth and blended.

Refrigerate any remaining sauce in an airtight container for up to 5 days.

Basic Stir-Fry Sauce

This sauce tastes like what you expect from a classic stir-fry sauce: salty, sweet, and tangy with a rich, nutty, and toasty taste from the sesame oil. The hot sauce also makes it a tad spicy, but it can be omitted (or decreased), if preferred.

Use this sauce to stir-fry vegetables, tofu, tempeh, chickpeas, or soy curls.

Makes about 1 cup

2 tablespoons dark soy sauce or soy sauce

2 tablespoons low-sodium tamari or soy sauce

¼ cup rice vinegar

2 teaspoons toasted sesame oil or sesame oil

2 teaspoons hot sauce

1 tablespoon plus 1 teaspoon maple syrup

2 teaspoons minced fresh ginger

½ teaspoon ground white pepper

2 teaspoons cornstarch

In a medium bowl, combine the dark soy sauce, tamari, rice vinegar, sesame oil, hot sauce, maple syrup, ginger, white pepper, cornstarch, and 4 teaspoons water and mix well. Use immediately.

Add the sauce to the stir-fry towards the end of the cooking process and continue to cook just until warmed through.

Hoisin Stir-Fry Sauce

Hoisin sauce resembles barbecue sauce in taste but is saltier, richer, and less sweet. Intensely flavored and versatile, it's often used in stir-fry dishes. It can be a little expensive but it's worth every penny. I've yet to create a good homemade substitute.

Use this sauce to stir-fry vegetables, tofu, tempeh, chickpeas, or soy curls.

Makes about ¾ cup

⅓ cup low-sodium soy sauce or tamari

3 tablespoons maple syrup

1½ tablespoons chili-garlic sauce

1½ tablespoons hoisin sauce

1½ tablespoons toasted sesame oil

In a medium bowl, whisk the soy sauce, maple syrup, chili-garlic sauce, hoisin sauce, and toasted sesame oil until smooth and blended.

Add this sauce to your stir-fry towards the end of the cooking process and continue to cook just until warmed through.

Sesame
Stir-Fry
Sauce

Toasted sesame oil adds an intense sesame flavor, making this a rich and delicious sauce. Sriracha adds a spicy kick but can be reduced or eliminated for a less spicy version.

Use this sauce to stir-fry vegetables, tofu, tempeh, chickpeas, or soy curls.

Makes about 1 cup

¼ cup **low-sodium soy sauce or tamari**

2 tablespoons **rice vinegar**

1 tablespoon **sriracha**

1½ teaspoons **toasted sesame oil**

1½ to 2 tablespoons **maple syrup**, or to taste

1 tablespoon **cornstarch**

In a medium bowl, mix together the soy sauce, rice vinegar, sriracha, toasted sesame oil, and ¼ cup water. Add 1½ tablespoons maple syrup and adjust to taste. Whisk in the cornstarch until fully dissolved. Use immediately.

Add this sauce to your stir-fry towards the end of the cooking process and continue to cook just until warmed through.

Peanut
Sauce

Fiery and tangy chili-garlic sauce paired with nutty sweet-and-salty peanut butter is nothing short of amazing.

Use this as a dipping sauce for crudités. Or serve it warm with Chickpea Croutons (page 222), Crispy Baked Tofu Cubes (page 213), Soy Curls (page 218), pan-fried tempeh, or noodles. It can also be used in a stir-fry.

Makes about ⅔ cup

¼ cup **low-sodium soy sauce or tamari**

1 tablespoon plus 1 teaspoon **rice vinegar**

⅓ cup **smooth peanut, almond, or cashew butter**

1 tablespoon **chili-garlic sauce**

1 tablespoon **maple syrup**

2 tablespoons **sesame oil**

In a medium bowl, mix the soy sauce, rice vinegar, peanut butter, chili-garlic sauce, maple syrup, and sesame oil until smooth. (You can also combine these ingredients in a blender and blend until smooth.)

To use in a stir-fry: Add the desired amount of sauce to the stir-fry towards the end of the cooking process and continue to cook just until warmed through.

Refrigerate any remaining sauce in an airtight container for up to 3 days.

Practically Vegan

Sweet & Spicy Gingery Stir-Fry Sauce

This sauce brings together all my favorite stir-fry sauce ingredients in one recipe, so you can imagine just how flavorful it is. It contains dark soy sauce, which is aged longer than regular soy sauce, making it richer, thicker, and darker in color. If you don't have dark soy sauce, it can be swapped for regular soy sauce. It will still be incredibly tasty, but slightly toned down in flavor.

Use this sauce to stir-fry vegetables, tofu, tempeh, chickpeas, or soy curls.

Makes about ¾ cup

3 tablespoons **coconut aminos**

1 tablespoon **dark soy sauce or soy sauce**

2 tablespoons **low-sodium tamari or soy sauce**, plus more as needed

3 tablespoons **maple syrup**

2 tablespoons **rice vinegar**

2 tablespoons **toasted sesame oil**

2 teaspoons **sriracha**

2 teaspoons minced **fresh ginger**

2 **garlic cloves**, minced

1 tablespoon **cornstarch**

In a small bowl, mix together the coconut aminos, dark soy sauce, tamari, maple syrup, rice vinegar, toasted sesame oil, sriracha, ginger, and garlic. In a separate small bowl, dissolve the cornstarch in 1 tablespoon water to make a slurry.

Add the sauce and the slurry to the stir-fry towards the end of the cooking process. Cook over low heat until the sauce starts to thicken and is warmed through. Serve immediately.

Teriyaki Sauce

½ cup **low-sodium soy sauce or tamari**

1½ teaspoons **chili-garlic sauce**

¼ cup **rice vinegar**

2 tablespoons plus 2 teaspoons **maple syrup**

2 teaspoons **mirin**

1½ teaspoons **sriracha**

4 **garlic cloves**, minced

1½ teaspoons minced **fresh ginger**

2 teaspoons **cornstarch** (optional, for a thicker sauce)

This sweet, tangy, sticky sauce delivers a big punch of salty umami. It contains mirin, a sweet-salty Japanese cooking wine that is a key ingredient in teriyaki sauce. Mirin is very versatile and can be added to most stir-fry sauces and marinades.

Use this sauce in a stir-fry, or with some of the Protein Sides in chapter 7 (pages 211–222).

Makes about 1 cup

In a medium bowl, mix the soy sauce, chili-garlic sauce, rice vinegar, maple syrup, mirin, sriracha, garlic, and ginger. For a thicker sauce, in a small bowl, mix the cornstarch with 1 tablespoon plus 1 teaspoon water until it dissolves fully. Add the cornstarch slurry to the medium bowl with the sauce ingredients.

Cooking method 1 *(with a protein side, such as Chickpea Croutons, page 222; Crispy Baked Tofu Cubes, page 213; and Soy Curls, page 218):* Add the desired amount of sauce to the skillet with the protein side. Cook over medium-low heat until the sauce starts to caramelize and stick to the bottom of the skillet.

Cooking method 2 *(for a stir-fry):* Add the sauce towards the end of the cooking process and continue to cook over medium-high heat. Once the sauce starts to bubble, reduce the heat to low and continue to cook until it just starts to stick to the base of the saucepan.

Ketchup

Store-bought ketchup is often loaded with sugar and salt. Making your own allows you to adjust the ingredients for a healthier version.

¼ cup tomato paste

2 tablespoons maple syrup

2 tablespoons apple cider vinegar

1 teaspoon sriracha or hot sauce (optional)

1 teaspoon low-sodium tamari or soy sauce

Salt to taste

Makes about ½ cup

In a medium bowl, whisk together the tomato paste, maple syrup, cider vinegar, sriracha (if using), and tamari. Add salt to taste.

Refrigerate any leftover ketchup in an airtight container for up to 3 days.

BBQ Sauce

This tangy, slightly sweet barbecue sauce packs a ton of flavor using an array of spices you typically find in chili.

It pairs perfectly with Chickpea Croutons (page 222), Crispy Baked Tofu Cubes (page 213), Crispy Tofu Cutlets (page 217), Chickpea Fritters (page 129), Tempeh Nuggets (page 219), Cornflake-Crusted Tofu (page 214), and pan-fried tempeh.

3 tablespoons apple cider vinegar

1 tablespoon freshly squeezed lemon juice

1 tablespoon maple syrup

1 tablespoon vegan Worcestershire sauce

1 tablespoon Dijon mustard

1 to 2 tablespoons ketchup, store-bought or homemade (above), or to taste

½ teaspoon smoked paprika

½ teaspoon chili powder

½ teaspoon onion powder

½ teaspoon garlic powder

½ teaspoon finely ground black pepper

Salt to taste

Makes about ½ cup

In a small bowl, mix together the cider vinegar, lemon juice, maple syrup, Worcestershire, mustard, ketchup, smoked paprika, chili powder, onion powder, garlic powder, and black pepper. Season with salt.

Refrigerate any leftover sauce in an airtight container for up to 3 days.

Acknowledgments

I wrote my first book during a pandemic. I never thought I'd write a book, let alone in a pandemic. I mean, who would?

This book was my saving grace in 2020. I signed the contract in April, just when COVID-19 was raging in New York City. I felt so lucky to be given the opportunity to write a cookbook, especially at a time when all I wanted to do was cook my blues away. Thank you, Alison Fargis, my fierce, one-of-a-kind agent, and the warm and welcoming team at Rodale, for being certain about me even at a time of so much uncertainty. You made this happen.

Thank you to:

Jonathan Safran Foer, for believing in me and planting the seed for this cookbook. If you hadn't so generously offered to write the foreword, I would never have written it. You are why I can now call myself an author.

Naya, Nikita, and Asha, my three kind and resilient daughters, for being such adventurous eaters and trusting me when I encouraged you to eat your vegetables. Not many teens would have tested every single recipe for a vegan cookbook, even the ones that flopped and never made it in.

My dad, who continues to eat the entire banana, peel included, for constantly reminding me of my strengths along the way, every single time I doubted myself.

Kim-Julie Hansen (@bestofvegan), one of the pioneers of building a vegan community on social media, for supporting me and helping me grow my social media presence when nobody knew who I was. You, telling me to read Jonathan's book *We Are the Weather*, is how this all began.

Dana Gallagher, for producing one amazing photo after another. You soldiered through and met the deadline despite it being a very difficult time in your life.

Cyd McDowell, the most gifted food stylist in the whole world, for taking on this project at the last minute and still managing to make everything look so delicious, all while standing over a hot stove, wearing a mask.

My diligent and generous recipe testers: Amina Sirry, the Fong family, Sara Silberman, Jennifer Kurani, Sanjana Samtani, Varsha Mahtani, Bindya Lulla, Deepa Massand-Vaswani, Aarti Kamat, Barbara Deli, Raam Melvani, and Siobhan Haber.

The Rodale team for making my cookbook more beautiful than I could have ever imagined: My brilliant editor, Dervla Kelly, for telling me I was strong and beautiful and never commenting on my poor sentence structure. Art director Stephanie Huntwork, for all the inspired creativity and for accepting my many quirks, like not wanting water glasses in the photos! (As you can see, I gave in!) Awesome designer Ian Dingman, who graciously acknowledged all my design requests and made them happen. The copy editor, Kathy Brock, who went through this entire manuscript with as fine-toothed a comb as I could ever have imagined and found all my mistakes (I hope). Huge thanks also to production editor Abby Oladipo, indexer Elizabeth Parson, editorial assistant Katherine Leak, production manager Kim Tyner, proofreader Rachel Holzman, and compositors Merri Ann Morrell and Zoe Tokushige.

Index